LITERATURE GUIDE

GCSE

Lord of the Flies

First published 2003
exclusively for WHSmith by
Hodder & Stoughton Educational
338 Euston Road
London
NW1 3BH

ISBN 0 340 87288 8

Illustrations: Karen Donnelly
Mind Maps ®: Anne Jones

Typeset by Transet Limited, Leamington Spa, England.
Printed in Great Britain for Hodder & Stoughton Educational, a division of
Hodder Headline Plc, 338 Euston Road, London NW1 3BH by Cox & Wyman
Ltd., Reading, Berkshire.

CONTENTS

MEMORY

There are five important things you must know about your brain and memory to revolutionise the way you study:

◆ how your memory ('recall') works *while* you are learning
◆ how your memory works *after* you have finished learning
◆ how to use Mind Maps – a special technique for helping you with all aspects of your studies
◆ how to increase your reading speed
◆ how to prepare for tests and exams.

Recall during learning
– THE NEED FOR BREAKS

When you are studying, your memory can concentrate, understand and remember well for between 20 and 45 minutes at a time. Then it needs a break. If you carry on for longer than this without a break your memory starts to break down. If you study for hours non-stop, you will remember only a small fraction of what you have been trying to learn, and you will have wasted hours of valuable time.

So, ideally, *study for less than an hour*, then take a five to ten minute break. During the break listen to music, go for a walk, do some exercise, or just daydream. (Daydreaming is a necessary brain-power booster – geniuses do it regularly.) During the break your brain will be sorting out what it has been learning, and you will go back to your books with the new information safely stored and organised in your memory banks. We recommend breaks at regular intervals as you work through the Literature Guides. Make sure you take them!

Recall after learning
– THE WAVES OF YOUR MEMORY

What do you think begins to happen to your
memory straight after you have finished learning something?
Does it immediately start forgetting? No! Your brain actually
increases its power and carries on remembering. For a short
time after your study session, your brain integrates the
information, making a more complete picture of everything it
has just learnt. Only then does the rapid decline in memory
begin, and as much as 80 per cent of what you have learnt can
be forgotten in a day.

However, if you catch the top of the wave of your memory, and
briefly review (look back over) what you have been studying at
the correct time, the memory is stamped in far more strongly,
and stays at the crest of the wave for a much longer time. To
maximise your brain's power to remember, take a few minutes
and use a Mind Map to review what you have learnt at the end
of a day. Then review it at the end of a week, again at the end
of a month, and finally a week before your test or exam. That
way you'll ride your memory wave
all the way there – and beyond!

The Mind Map ®
– A PICTURE OF THE WAY YOU THINK

Do you like taking notes? More importantly, do you like having to
go back over and learn them before tests or exams? Most
students I know certainly do not! And how do you take your
notes? Most people take notes on lined paper, using blue or
black ink. The result, visually, is boring! And what does *your* brain
do when it is bored? It turns off, tunes out, and goes to sleep!
Add a dash of colour, rhythm, imagination, and the whole note-
taking process becomes much more fun, uses more of your
brain's abilities, and improves your recall and understanding.

A Mind Map mirrors the way your brain works. It can be used
for note-taking from books or in class, for reviewing what you
have just studied, and for essay planning for coursework and in
tests or exams. It uses all your memory's natural techniques to
build up your rapidly growing 'memory muscle'.

You will find Mind Maps throughout this book. Study them, add some colour, personalise them, and then have a go at drawing your own – you'll remember them far better! Stick them in your files and on your walls for a quick-and-easy review of the topic.

HOW TO DRAW A MIND MAP

1 Start in the middle of the page. This gives your brain the maximum room for its thoughts.
2 Always start by drawing a small picture or symbol. Why? Because a picture is worth a thousand words to your brain. And try to use at least three colours, as colour helps your memory even more.
3 Let your thoughts flow, and write or draw your ideas on coloured branching lines connected to your central image. These key symbols and words are the headings for your topic. Start like the Mind Map on page 8.
4 Then add facts and ideas by drawing more, smaller, branches on to the appropriate main branches, just like a tree.
5 Always print your word clearly on its line. Use only one word per line.
6 To link ideas and thoughts on different branches, use arrows, colours, underlining, and boxes (see page 12).

HOW TO READ A MIND MAP

1 Begin in the centre, the focus of your topic.
2 The words/images attached to the centre are like chapter headings, read them next.
3 Always read out from the centre, in every direction (even on the left-hand side, where you will have to read from right to left, instead of the usual left to right).

USING MIND MAPS

Mind Maps are a versatile tool – use them for taking notes in class or from books, for solving problems, for brainstorming with friends, and for reviewing and working for tests or exams – their uses are endless! You will find them invaluable for planning essays for coursework and exams. Number your main branches in the order in which you want to use them and off you go – the main headings for your essay are done and all your ideas are logically organised!

Super speed reading

It seems incredible, but it's been proved – the faster you read, the more you understand and remember! So here are some tips to help you to practise reading faster – you'll cover the ground more quickly, remember more, and have more time left for both work and play.

◆ First read the whole text (whether it's a lengthy book or an exam or test paper) very quickly, to give your brain an overall idea of what's ahead and get it working. (It's like sending out a scout to look at the territory you have to cover – it's much easier when you know what to expect!) Then read the text again for more detailed information.

◆ Have the text a reasonable distance away from your eyes. In this way your eye/brain system will be able to see more at a glance, and will naturally begin to read faster.

◆ Take in groups of words at a time. Rather than reading 'slowly and carefully' read faster, more enthusiastically.

◆ Take in phrases rather than single words while you read.

◆ Use a guide. Your eyes are designed to follow movement, so a thin pencil underneath the lines you are reading, moved smoothly along, will 'pull' your eyes to faster speeds.

Preparing for tests and exams

◆ Review your work systematically. Cram at the start of your course, not the end, and avoid 'exam panic'!

◆ Use Mind Maps throughout your course, and build a Master Mind Map for each subject – a giant Mind Map that summarises everything you know about the subject.

◆ Use memory techniques such as mnemonics (verses or systems for remembering things like dates and events).

◆ Get together with one or two friends to study, compare Mind Maps, and discuss topics.

AND FINALLY...

Have *fun* while you learn – it has been shown that students who make their studies enjoyable understand and remember everything better and get the highest grades. I wish you and your brain every success! (Tony Buzan)

HOW TO USE THIS GUIDE

This guide assumes that you have already read *Lord of the Flies*, although you could read 'Background' and 'The story of *Lord of the Flies*' before that. It is best to use the guide alongside the text. You could read the 'Who's who?' and 'Themes' sections without referring to the novel, but you will get more out of these sections if you do refer to it to check the points made, and especially when thinking about the questions designed to test your recall and help you think about the novel.

The different sections

The 'Commentary' section can be used in a number of ways. One way is to read a chapter or part of a chapter in the novel, and then read the commentary for that section. Keep on until you come to a test yourself exercise – then have a break! Alternatively, read the commentary for a chapter or part of a chapter, then read that section in the novel, then go back to the commentary. Find out what works best for you.

'Topics for discussion and brainstorming' gives topics that could well feature in exams or provide the basis for coursework. It would be particularly useful for you to discuss them with friends, or brainstorm them using Mind Map techniques (see p. v).

'How to get an "A" in English Literature' gives valuable advice on what to look for in any text, and what skills you need to develop in order to achieve your personal best.

'The exam essay' is a useful 'night before' reminder of how to tackle exam questions, and 'Model answer' gives an example of an A-grade essay and the Mind Map and plan used to write it.

The questions

Whenever you come across a question in the guide with a star
❂ in front of it, think about it for a moment. You could even jot
down a few words in rough to focus your mind. There is not
usually a 'right' answer to these questions: it is important for
you to develop your own opinions if you want to get an 'A'.
The 'Test yourself' sections are designed to take you about
10–20 minutes each – which will be time well spent. Take a
short break after each one.

Page numbers

Page references are to the Penguin Modern Classics edition. If
you have another edition, the page numbers may be slightly
different, although the chapters will be the same.

KEY TO ICONS

Themes and imagery

A **theme** is an idea explored by an author. **Imagery** refers to the kind of word picture used to make the idea come alive. Particular sorts of image are usually associated with each theme. Whenever a theme is dealt with in the guide, the appropriate icon is used. This means you can find where a theme is dealt with just by flicking through the book.
Go on – try it now!

Evil

Power/leadership

Order

Nature/island

Savagery

STYLE AND LANGUAGE

This heading and icon are used in the Commentary wherever there is a special section on the author's choice of words and use of literary devices.

BACKGROUND

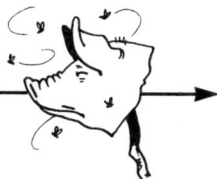

Lord of the Flies was first published in 1954. Its author, William Golding, was born in Cornwall in 1911, and brought up in Wiltshire. His father was a teacher and a socialist and his mother actively supported the campaign for votes for women, so from an early age he was aware of social and political systems and their influence on people.

Influences on the book

During the Second World War Golding joined the Royal Navy and took part in the sinking of the Bismark and the Normandy landings on D-Day. His experience of the war had a profound effect on his view of the world. It taught him just how brutal people could be to each other. Although he was appalled by the evils of Nazism and the Third Reich, he said in an interview in 1963 that everyone was capable of inhumanity, not just the German or the Japanese. He saw Nazism as an evil political system, and so horrifying that it could not be explained through reason alone. He looked for an explanation in the nature of human beings, in their capacity for brutality and inhumanity.

These are some of the ideas he explores in Lord of the Flies. Golding was familiar with adventure stories such as Coral Island – he read them to his children – and wondered what would really happen to children stranded on a desert island. He took the idea of an innocent experience on an island and saw it in relation to the experience of Nazism and World War Two.

Parallels to be made

Because of this, Lord of the Flies can be read on different levels. In some ways it is an **allegory** – a story which has a literal meaning and a symbolic meaning. There are ways in which the novel parallels the rise of Hitler, or the rise of any dictator. You may wish to see some of the characters in the novel as representing certain historical figures or types. Another aspect of the Lord of the Flies is the use of **myth** and **fable**. A myth is an ancient traditional story of gods and heroes, which has evolved over time, and which embodies popular ideas and beliefs. A fable is a story with a specific moral or message, usually made up by one person (e.g. Aesop). *Lord of the Flies* has elements of both these types of story. You will see some biblical parallels in the depiction of Simon as a Christ-like figure and the island as the Garden of Eden, where the snake is evil and human beings' innocence is stained by sin. The message of the story is that the evil is a powerful presence whose influence in us all must be recognised.

William Golding received the Nobel Prize for Literature in 1983 and he died in 1993.

now study the Mind Map opposite which outlines the plot of the book

3

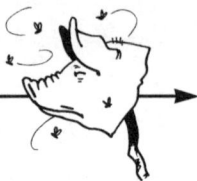

Setting the scene

The story begins as a **plane** evacuating children from a war zone crashes on a remote **island** in the tropics. The only survivors are a group of boys. There is **Ralph**, **Piggy**, the members of a choir school led by **Jack**, and an assortment of others of different ages. They are brought together when Ralph and Piggy find a **conch** shell and Ralph blows it. They elect Ralph to be **leader** of the group and he lets Jack be in charge of the **choir**. Jack decides his choir will be hunters. Ralph, Jack and Simon (one of the choir) explore the island and find that it is uninhabited.

Getting organised

The boys have regular meetings. Whoever holds the **conch** has the right to **speak**. Some of the little boys talk about being scared of a **beast** they think they see at night. They agree to build shelters to sleep in and to keep a **fire** burning on the mountain, to give a smoke signal. Jack says his hunters will be responsible for keeping the fire going. They realise one of the small boys is missing, probably dead.

Ralph and a few others build shelters while Jack and his group hunt. They let the fire go out. A **ship** passes but there is no smoke. When the hunters return with the **pig** they have killed there is a bitter argument between the two groups. Jack's group acts out the killing as a ritual **ceremony**. This becomes a part of the hunt.

Things go wrong

Most of the boys begin to behave irresponsibly, and **Jack** refuses to **obey** the rules. They talk about 'the beast' and being scared. A **pilot** dies parachuting on to the mountain. The boys think this figure is the beast and are terrified. Jack breaks away from Ralph and forms his own group, which becomes a tribe of savages. They kill a pig and leave its **head** as an offering for the beast.

Death and rescue

Simon sees the **head** on a stick and has an imaginary **conversation** with it. He climbs the **mountain** to find out what the 'beast' really is. As he comes down the mountain to tell the others what he has found, all the others, having had a huge feast, are performing a ritual **dance**. They think Simon is the beast and attack and **kill** him.

Ralph's group is now very **small** and finds it hard to keep the **fire** going. Jack's tribe raids them to **steal** Piggy's **glasses** to light their fire. Ralph's group goes to ask Jack for Piggy's glasses back. As they confront Jack's tribe, Piggy is killed and Jack attacks Ralph. Ralph's last two **supporters** are taken **prisoner**. Ralph escapes and hides in the forest. Jack and his tribe **hunt** Ralph, intending to **kill** him. They roll rocks, then set fire to the island to **smoke** him out. A passing **ship** sees this smoke and pulls in to **rescue** the boys.

HOW WELL HAVE YOU REMEMBERED THE PLOT?

Fill in the keywords in the blanks overleaf without looking back. Then check how you've done.

Setting the scene

The story begins as a _____ evacuating children from a war zone crashes on a remote_____ in the tropics. The only survivors are a group of boys. There is_____, _____, the members of a choir school led by_____, and an assortment of others of different ages. They are brought together when Ralph and Piggy find a _____ shell and Ralph blows it. They elect Ralph to be _____ of the group and he lets Jack be in charge of the _____. Jack decides his choir will be hunters. Ralph, Jack and Simon (one of the choir) explore the island and find that it is uninhabited.

Getting organised

The boys have regular meetings. Whoever holds the_____ has the right to _____. Some of the little boys talk about being scared of a _____ they think they see at night. They agree to build shelters to sleep in and to keep a _____ burning on the mountain, to give a smoke signal. Jack says his hunters will be responsible for keeping the fire going. They realise one of the small boys is missing, probably dead.

Ralph and a few others build shelters while Jack and his group hunt. They let the fire go out. A _____ passes but there is no smoke. When the hunters return with the_____ they have killed there is a bitter argument between the two groups. Jack's group acts out the killing as a ritual _____. This becomes a part of the hunt.

Things go wrong

Most of the boys begin to behave irresponsibly and _____ refuses to_____the rules. They talk about 'the beast' and being scared. A _____dies parachuting onto the mountain. The boys think this figure is the beast and are terrified. Jack breaks away from Ralph and forms his own group,which becomes a tribe of savages. They kill a pig and leave its _____as an offering for the beast.

Death and rescue

_____ sees the_____on a stick and has an imaginary_____ with it. He climbs the_____ to find out what the 'beast' really is. As he comes down the mountain to tell the others what he has found, all the others, having had a huge feast, are performing a ritual_____ They think Simon is the beast and attack and _____ him.

Ralph's group is now very_____ and finds it hard to keep the_____ going. Jack's tribe raids them to_____ Piggy's glasses to light their fire. Ralph's group goes to ask Jack for Piggy's glasses back. As they confront Jack's tribe, Piggy is killed and Jack attacks Ralph. Ralph's last two_____ are taken prisoner. Ralph escapes and hides in the forest. Jack and his tribe _____Ralph, intending to_____ him. They roll rocks, then set fire to the island to_____ him out. A passing_____ sees this smoke and pulls in to_____ the boys.

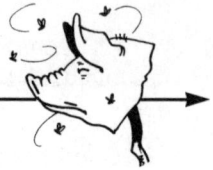

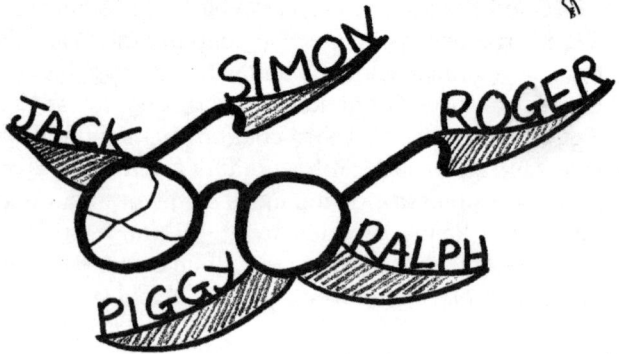

Ralph

Ralph is dependable and responsible. He is basically kind, with *a mildness about his mouth and eyes* (p. 10), and is a just and sensitive leader. His sensitivity can be seen in the way he deals with Jack's disappointment at losing the leadership vote by making him chief of the choir. He wants their society to operate in a democratic and civilised way and is distressed when things go wrong. Although intelligent, he often finds the tasks of thinking things through and making decisions too much for him, and relies on Piggy to help and prompt him. His respect for Piggy gradually increases as he grows to value Piggy's loyalty and common sense.

Ralph shows physical courage, such as when he forces himself to climb the mountain and face the beast, and moral courage in the way he admits his part in Simon's murder. He struggles to continue believing that people are fundamentally good. He can't understand how another boy like himself could experience real hatred: *'But he's, he's Jack Merridew!'* (p. 89). In the end he comes to recognise *the darkness of man's heart* (p. 192). Ralph represents the values of civilisation and democratic rule, which are eventually defeated by the evil contained within society.

Piggy

Piggy is an outsider. This is partly because of physical characteristics such as his plump body, his asthma (which would make energetic physical activity difficult for him) and his dislike of manual work, and partly because his common sense and scientific point of view make him an adult-type figure. His constant references to adults: *'What's grown-ups going to say?'* (p. 88) and to his auntie show his belief in the *majesty of adult life* (p. 90). Because of this he is often seen as a spoil-sport and a figure of fun. Piggy is more intelligent than Ralph, and has a deeper understanding of people than Ralph does. He recognises the hatred Jack feels.

Piggy shows unswerving loyalty to Ralph and to the end believes in the values represented by the conch. He can be morally dishonest, for example when he tries to explain away Simon's murder. He is also unimaginative: his staunch belief in the practical world of houses and streets and TVs makes him dismiss more intuitive responses to life, such as Simon's, and he is unable to understand the fear the others experience. However, although he has his limitations, Piggy's worthwhile qualities gradually emerge, and in the end he is seen courageously standing up for sense and rational behaviour.

Jack

Jack has a fierce and aggressive desire to lead and control. From the beginning he challenges Ralph's leadership and is obsessed with power. At the start he controls the *wearily obedient* (p. 20) choir with military discipline and at the end he rules his tribe of savages with the weapons of fear and torture. Jack rejects the democratic processes by which rules and decisions are made, and instead imposes his own desires by force. He overcomes and suppresses the civilised restraints which originally prevented him from killing a pig and surrenders himself to his violent and bloodthirsty instincts. He finds fulfilment in exercising power over others, which he does without any thought of justice or the people involved. His beating of Wilfred is a cruel abuse of his power. Jack finds primitive solutions to the problems on the island. He resorts to superstitious practices like leaving a sacrifice for the beast, and uses ritual to keep the tribe together and control their emotional responses.

Simon

Golding said that Simon is a *saint, a lover of mankind*. This is seen in Simon's behaviour as he performs acts of kindness such as helping the littluns to fruit and helping Ralph to build the shelters. Simon also has powers of vision and a kind of instinctive understanding of the world and the people in it. He is physically frail, suffering fits and faints, and is unable to communicate his insights. None of the others understands him, and he is dismissed as *batty* and *funny*. His response to the natural life of the island is different from that of the others, as we see when he retreats to his secret den and is absorbed by its richness and variety. Simon recognises that the real beast is in everyone, and that this truth must be accepted before we are either ruled by it or overcome it. Like martyrs who die for others, he is killed as he tries to tell the boys the truth about their situation.

Littluns

The littluns are the very young boys, aged about 6, who lead a *quite distinct* (p. 56) life of their own. They play and eat fruit which makes them ill, and suffer from fears and nightmares. They introduce the idea of the beast. We know one or two of them by name. Percival is a frightened little boy who is tormented by nightmares and pathetically recites his name and address like a charm that will protect him (p. 83). He is tormented by Johnny, another littlun who displays *natural belligerence* (p. 57), and Henry, whom we see absorbed in *exercising control over living things* as he prods sea-creatures with a stick (p. 58).

Roger

From the beginning Roger seems to be a sinister figure. He is a *slight, furtive boy* (p. 21) who always appears gloomy and brooding. His sadistic instincts are clear from when he throws stones at Henry, and they become unrestrained under Jack's rule. He becomes a killer and torturer, and excites more fear than Jack.

Sam and Eric

Sam and Eric are so similar that they are turned into one being, Samneric. (You might remember this as SAM + E = SAME.) They are good-natured cheerful boys who mean well and support Ralph, but are not strong enough to stand up to Jack. They want to do the right thing but don't have sufficient personal resources to defend civilised behaviour to the bitter end in the way that Ralph and Piggy do.

now that you are familiar with the main characters in the book, study the Mind Map on page 12 and then take a break

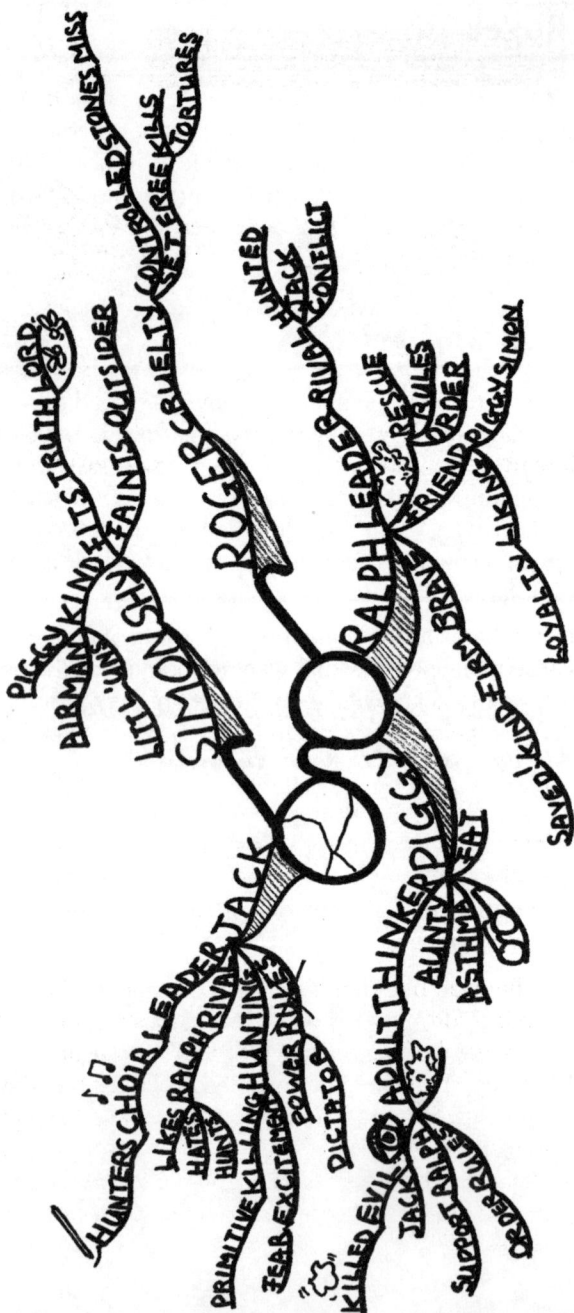

ROGER — CRUELTY — CONTROLLED — STONES MISS — SETS FREE — KILLS — TORTURES

RALPH — LEADER — RIVAL — HUNTED — ATTACK — CONFLICT — RESCUE — RULES — ORDER — FRIEND — PIGGY — SIMON — LIKEABLE — KIND — DESERT — LIKE KID — BRAVE — SAVED

SIMON — SHY — FAINTS — OUTSIDER — UNSURE — KIND — IT'S TRUTH — LORD — AIRMAN — PIGGY — LITTLE UN'S

JACK — LEADER — CHOIR — HUNTERS — LIKES RALPH — RIVAL — HATES — HUNT — HUNTING — PRIMITIVE — KILLING — FEAR — EXCITEMENT — POWER — RULES — DICTATOR — KILLED — EVIL — JACK — SUPPORT RALPH — ORDER RULES

PIGGY — ADULT — THINKER — AUNT — ASTHMA — FAT

12

THEMES

POWER · SAVAGERY · BEAST · ORDER · ISLAND

Evil

The evil that is inside human beings is personified in the beast. Because many people don't want to look inside themselves and don't want to acknowledge this aspect of their nature, they look for something external to be its cause or its embodiment.

This is what the boys do. On the island they are disturbed and frightened. They have lost all sense of home and security, and their nights are tormented by dreams and nightmares. At first they latch on to the idea that the branches are snakes, which they are frightened of. Then they imagine a beast which becomes the focal point of their fear.

When the dead pilot lands on the mountain top he becomes the physical form of the beast. Now they have a real figure, seen by several of the boys, which they can regard as a terrifying beast which can't be killed and must be appeased with offerings. Simon is the only one who sees this figure for what it really is, a corpse which is decomposing and becoming part of nature. The others look anywhere for the beast – the sea, the jungle, the mountain – rather than find it in themselves.

Order

The conch becomes a symbol for the world of order and civilisation. In the civilised culture from which the boys come, society is organised in a democratic way and there is a shared agreement about what is right and wrong and the way people should behave.

The boys' assemblies show their attempts to govern themselves according to these values. They try to establish and respect authority, and to impose order and discipline on their lives. This is seen as essential if they are to survive and be rescued. The conch is the precious emblem of this kind of order. Some of the characters respect the shell and what it represents to the end, while others challenge and finally dismiss it. When the conch is finally smashed, it signifies the end of order and civilisation on the island.

Savagery

The main descent to savagery in the novel may be seen in the choir. They begin as boys who accept the discipline of a choir school and acknowledge Jack's position as head chorister. They become hunters, as Jack claims this role for them. Then, as Jack releases his savage instincts by creating his mask, they become savages. They used to wear identical cloaks and caps, a uniform designed to promote their group identity and hide individuality. Now their identities are hidden by masks and paint, and they degenerate into a tribe of savage killers, living in fear of their cruel chief.

Every time they kill they take a step further down the road to savagery. The killing of the pigs becomes more bloodthirsty, and has more to do with ritual violence than with the providing of meat. The ritual of chanting and dancing increases in ferocity until it culminates in Simon's murder.

The final hunt in the novel is the hunt for Ralph. What they intend to do with his body shows how much they have changed. The echoes and reminders of playground games of chasing and hunting make the reality of what they are doing all the more sinister. In the end there is no element of civilisation left and the descent to savagery is complete.

Power/leadership

The main struggle for power is between Ralph and Jack. Each of them is a leader but the leadership each shows is based on different principles. Ralph's style of leadership is democratic and takes notice of others' opinions. He feels the responsibility of his position and also feels its burdens.

Jack's style of leadership is based on domination and fear. He imposes his will on others with no regard for their needs or feelings. He wields power without responsibility and exults in his domination over other beings, animal or human. What he can't dominate he seeks to destroy. Jack hides his own identity behind the anonymous title of Chief and the painted mask. With the protection of these trappings he is free to demonstrate the savage, brutal power which is the mark of his leadership.

Nature/island

The island is separate and isolated from the rest of the world. It is like a little world itself, a microcosm, which reflects what is happening in the great world outside. This is an unspoiled tropical island with an abundance of fruit and vegetation and natural life, and we may see some suggestion of the Garden of Eden. Nature on the island is beautiful, and at the same time potentially hostile. The fruit can refresh and also cause stomach aches; the heat can delight and also hit like a blow.

We can tell something about the different characters from their response to the island's natural life. Jack, for example, wants to exploit it to satisfy his own desires, whereas Simon is in sympathy with it and celebrates its beauty.

study the Mind Map on page 16 and then take a short break before going on to the Commentary

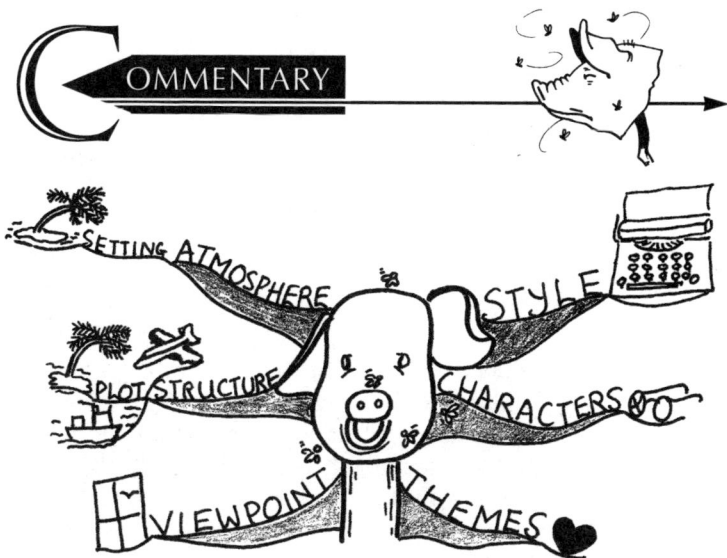

COMMENTARY

The Commentary divides the chapters into short sections, beginning with a brief preview which will prepare you for the section and help in last-minute revision. The Commentary comments on whatever is important in the section, focusing on the areas shown in the Mini Mind Map above.

Wherever there is a focus on a particular theme, the icon for that theme appears in the margin (see p. xi for key). Look out, too, for the 'Style and language' sections. Being able to comment on style and language will help you to get an 'A' in your exam.

USE YOUR NOVEL

You will learn more from the Commentary if you use it alongside the novel itself. Read a section from the novel, then the corresponding Commentary section – or the other way round.

Remember that when a question appears in the Commentary with a star ✪ in front of it, you should stop and think about it for a moment. And **remember** to take a break after completing each exercise!

Chapter 1   The Sound of the Shell

'What's your name?'

(To p. 15, *Something creamy lay among the ferny weeds.*)

◆ A group of boys is stranded on a desert island, following a plane crash.
◆ We meet: Ralph – 12 years old, fair-haired, athletic, confident; Piggy – short, fat, wears glasses, has asthma.

Ralph is delighted when he realises they are alone on the island and there are no grown-ups. He shows his delight by standing on his head. He strips off his clothes and swims in the warm sea, revelling in the heat and the exotic sights of the island. We learn that his father is a commander in the Navy and Ralph thinks he will rescue him from the island. He doesn't show much interest in Piggy. Look at the way he fails to respond when Piggy suggests calling a meeting, and doesn't ask Piggy his name in return. ❂ What do you think about Ralph's behaviour here? What does it tell you about him?

Piggy is alarmed when he realises there are no adults on the island. He is fat and unfit, and because he has asthma he isn't allowed to run or swim. He's been wearing glasses since he was three. He's been brought up by his auntie. He wants to be friends with Ralph in spite of Ralph's lack of interest. ❂ Why do you think Piggy confides his name to Ralph? Piggy thinks about their situation practically and realistically. ❂ Find some examples of this.

'It's a shell!'

(From p. 15, *A stone*, to p. 19, *and there was silence.*)

◆ They find a shell called a conch.
◆ Piggy tells Ralph how to blow it.
◆ The noise it makes brings boys from all directions.

Ralph and Piggy notice the creamy pink shell lying in the water. Ralph is lost in a day dream, feeling the island is like a dream come true. It's Piggy who knows what the shell is called and what sound it makes. Piggy suggests using it to call the others together, but he pretends to Ralph that it was Ralph's idea. ❂ Why do you think Piggy does this?

Your turn!

Stop now and take about 10 minutes to think about your first impressions of Piggy and Ralph. Use this chart to help you make some notes on the differences between them.

	Ralph	Piggy
social (home, school background)		
physical		
mental (how they think, react)		

before going on to see the effect of Jack's arrival, take a short break!

'Choir! Stand still!'

(From p. 19, *Within the diamond haze of the beach*, to p. 20, *... and busied himself with his glasses.*)

◆ The choir arrives.
◆ Jack – red-haired, freckled, blue-eyed, arrogant – leads them.
◆ Simon faints.

Jack first appears leading a column of marching choir boys. Despite the tropical heat they are wearing their uniform black caps and cloaks and seem almost like a well-disciplined army under Jack's command. We are told he *controlled* them and *shouted an order*. He lets them sit down only when Simon faints.

Simon often faints. This is the first thing which makes him seem different from the rest of the boys. ✪ How does Jack react to his fainting? Jack wants to be known by his surname only. ✪ Can you think why?

Ralph reveals Piggy's nickname although Piggy had asked him not to, and everyone laughs. Piggy is an outsider from the beginning. ✪ Are you surprised that Piggy is treated like this? Do you see him as someone to be made fun of?

'Vote for chief!'

(From p. 20, *Merridew turned to Ralph*, to p. 24, *He went back to the platform*.)

◆ They vote for chief and Ralph is elected.
◆ Ralph makes Jack leader of the choir.
◆ Jack says the choir will be hunters.

Jack thinks he ought to be chief. ✪ What reasons does he give? Do you think they are good reasons? Piggy and Ralph are the other possibilities. Look at the things which influence the boys' choice and by each statement give a mark out of 10 for how important **you** think it is, and a mark out of 10 for how important **the boys** think it is.

	me	the boys
Piggy has shown intelligence		
Jack is an obvious leader		
Ralph looks attractive		
Ralph blew the conch		
Ralph is holding the conch		
✪ Do you think they made the right choice?		

The first time the conch is blown shows the beginning of order on the island. It is the sign for them to come together and start to organise themselves. From the beginning it is associated with authority and democracy.

Ralph offers Jack the choir and lets him decide what they should be. This is his first action as chief. ✪ Why does he do this? Does he think what the consequences might be? He then makes his first speech as chief.

Here are some key words from Ralph's speech: *think, decide, rescue.* ✪ What kind of leader do you think he will be?

Ralph chooses Jack and Simon to explore the island with him. Piggy shows Ralph that he is hurt at being left out, and was also hurt and humiliated when Ralph told the others his name. Ralph recognises Piggy's feelings and responds *with the directness of genuine leadership.* He gives Piggy the job of staying behind to collect names.

Over to you!

Use the questions on the next page to make some notes about what happens each time the conch is blown. Make a Mind Map if you prefer.

- Who blows the conch?
- Why does he blow it?
- Does it bring order or chaos?
- Who respects it?
- Who ignores it?

Now take 10 minutes to think about Jack and the differences between him and Ralph. What kind of person is Jack? Look at the way he treats the choir and the way they respond to him. Look at the way he treats Piggy. Is it the same as the way as Ralph treats Piggy? What does his appearance suggest – his black cloak and his red hair? Use the chart to make notes of your ideas. Jot down words, pictures, signs.

	Jack	Ralph
appearance		
attitude to other people		
way of talking and behaving		

now take a short break before going on to the final part of the chapter

'This belongs to us!'

(From p. 24, *The three boys walked briskly on the sand*, to end of chapter.)

◆ Ralph, Jack and Simon explore the island.
◆ They climb to the highest point.
◆ They find a piglet trapped in creepers.
◆ Jack draws a knife to kill it but can't bring himself to.

The island is tropical and unspoiled. The shore is lined with a terrace of palm trees and the forest stretches behind. It is marked by the 'scar' left by the aircraft when it crashed before being dragged out to sea. A mile away from the shore is a coral reef, forming a lagoon between it and the island. A four foot high platform of pink granite rises out of the forest, beach and water. On one side of it a beach pool has formed.

Although the island is beautiful, some of the words Golding uses suggest a darker side. The coconuts are *decaying* and *skull-like*. ✪ The fruit is lovely – but what effect has it had on most of the boys?

The three boys make their way through the forest and climb to the top of the mountain. They find out that it is definitely an island and that it is uninhabited. At the other end of it they see a rock, like a fort. They are thrilled and excited by the glamour of the island, and the idea of having it all to themselves. Ralph shows his feelings by standing on his head again. On the way up Jack gets them to heave a huge rock into the forest below. ✪ Why do you think he does this?

Coming down the mountain they find some bushes with green buds. Look at the different way they react to them.
✪ Think of images to remind you of the three boys' different responses. Simon says they're like candles. Think about the words and places associated with candles – they burn in churches or places of worship, they bring light in the darkness. ✪ What does this suggest about the kind of person Simon is?

Jack is furious with himself when he can't kill the piglet. Look at the way he slams the knife into the tree trunk and looks at them fiercely as he says he will do it next time. Now he has something to prove – but at the moment he is still influenced by the ideas and customs of civilised society.

STYLE AND LANGUAGE

As you have worked through this chapter you will have become aware of the way language can create lots of different ideas and associations. The beauty of the island is conveyed through descriptive phrases like *the lagoon was still as a mountain lake – blue of all shades and shadowy green and purple.* There are also words and phrases that suggest evil and destruction. Look at phrases like *smashed a deep hole in the canopy of the forest,* and the references to a bomb and a machine-gun. Remember that elsewhere there is a war going on. These phrases **foreshadow** (i.e. warn us of) what is to come. Find some more examples of phrases which express the island's beauty, and of phrases which suggest something darker.

Try this!

See what you can recall about the appearance of the conch. Without looking at the text, insert the missing words in this passage. If you can't recall the exact words, use appropriate alternatives.

In colour the shell was_____, touched here and there with _____ pink. Between the point worn away into a little hole, and the _____, _____ of the mouth lay eighteen inches of shell with a slight _____ twist and covered with a _____, embossed _____.

Compare your words with the original.

Finally, use this map of the island to help you keep track of the story. You will find it at the end of some chapter commentaries. One or two items have been filled in. Use lines or arrows to trace the journey made in this chapter, and add any illustrations or notes you want to.

now that you're familiar with the main characters, take a break!

Chapter 2   Fire on the Mountain

Fun and rescue

(To p. 34, *Apparently no one had found anything.*)

◆ Ralph calls a meeting to report back what they have found.
◆ Making rules.

Ralph blows the conch to bring everyone together. He explains that the island is uninhabited and that there aren't any grown-ups so they will have to look after themselves. He says that they will need hunters to get meat. He decides that anyone who wants to speak must put his hand up for the conch, and that everyone has the right to speak without interruption while holding it. ✪ Why is it important that there are no adults on the island? What are the advantages and disadvantages of using the conch?

Jack says again that he will kill the pig next time. He is excited by the idea of rules and interrupts Ralph. ✪ What does Jack's behaviour suggest about his attitude to rules? What will he do to people who break them?

Piggy takes the conch and points out that they might be on the island for a long time. Look at the way he supports Ralph, and how he pretends that his ideas are Ralph's. Ralph tells them all that the island is good, and that they can have fun while waiting to be rescued. The boys compare the island to ones they've read about in adventure books.

Beast on the island

(From p. 34, *The older boys first noticed,* to p. 36, *The assembly was silent.*)

◆ Small boy with mulberry coloured birthmark speaks.
◆ He's frightened of a beastie or snake-thing.

◆ Ralph says it doesn't exist.
◆ Jack says they'll hunt it and kill it.

The little boy says he's scared of a beastie that turns into one of the jungle creepers during the day but becomes a snake or beast at night. Notice how Piggy encourages him to speak and interprets what he says. The younger boys aren't easily convinced that it was just a dream or a nightmare. ❂ What is your interpretation of the beast? You've already looked at the way Golding has suggested a dark side to this island. ❂ How might the beast be part of this?

'We must make a fire'

(From p. 36, *Ralph lifted the conch*, to p. 38, *over the tumbled scar*.)

◆ Ralph talks about rescue.
◆ They need to keep a fire going on the top of the mountain.
◆ The boys rush up the mountain to get wood.
◆ Jack leads.
◆ Ralph and Piggy follow.

Ralph tells them that he's been thinking about their situation and he's certain the grown-ups will rescue them. He has confidence in his father and in the idea that the Queen will have a picture of their island. ❂ Why do you think the boys applaud when he says this? Look at the way Ralph finds it difficult to hold a train of thought. This is one of the things he will find difficult about being leader. ❂ What other difficulties does he face at this point?

Ralph has worked out that they must have a fire on top of the mountain to give a smoke signal to any ships that might pass. As soon as Ralph says this, the boys rush off up the mountain, following Jack. Piggy is scornful of their behaviour and says they are acting *'like a crowd of kids'*. ❷ Why doesn't Piggy think of himself as a 'kid'? Notice that they leave the conch behind, but Piggy strokes it *respectfully* and carries it to the mountain.

Over to you

Take 10 minutes now to add to your ideas about Ralph and Piggy and Jack. Look at how they behave in the passages you've just read and decide which character the following words and phrases are linked with. You can apply them to more than one character.

Ralph   **Piggy**   **Jack**

democracy   hunting   naive   order   reassuring
punishment   loyal   optimistic   realistic   scared
excited   obsessed   responsible   kind   authority

there's no smoke without fire. Find out more after you take a break!

Building the fire

(From p. 38, *Below the other side of the mountain*, to p. 43, *'You got your small fire all right.'*)

◆ They build a huge pile of dead wood.
◆ No matches.
◆ Jack snatches Piggy's glasses to light the fire.
◆ Fire creates lots of flames but no smoke.

The boys make a great pile of dry, rotten wood as Piggy remains apart. When they realise they have no means of lighting the fire, Jack grabs Piggy's glasses off his face to use as a focus for the heat of the sun. Piggy needs his glasses and is terrified when Jack does this. ✪ In what ways is Piggy weak, and in what ways is he strong? He points out that the fire isn't any good and Jack turns on him with contempt, telling him to shut up. Jack also says that the rule about the conch doesn't count on top of the mountain, but Ralph supports Piggy and says the conch counts everywhere. Look at the way Jack then talks about the importance of keeping the rules and doing the right things. ✪ Do you think Jack means what he says? Why do you think he is so hostile to Piggy? Piggy knows that although he speaks sense the others don't listen to him.

Where is he now?

✪ What does he feel about this? Why isn't he listened to?

(From p. 43, *Smoke was rising here and there*, to end of chapter.)

◆ The fire gets out of control.
◆ Piggy tells them how irresponsible they've been.
◆ The little boy with the birthmark is missing.

The fire rages through a quarter mile square of forest. Piggy is very angry when the boys giggle at what they've done. Notice that although he complains that people don't take notice of what he says, when he feels strongly about something he's not afraid to speak out. He insists on his right to speak when he's holding the conch. He points out that they should have made shelters, that they should have built a proper fire, that they don't give Ralph time to think, and that they should know how many littluns there were. Piggy realises that the boy with the mulberry-coloured birth mark is missing. This is the first death on the island; he has presumably died in the fire they have made, and is never seen again.

STYLE AND LANGUAGE

Look at the **imagery** (word pictures) used to describe the fire. Golding uses **metaphors** (describing the fire as if it's something else – an animal) and **similes**. (Similes compare one thing to something else that is different in most ways but similar in one important way.) He compares the fire to an animal. At first it's like a *bright squirrel*, but it becomes a *kind of wildlife* which *crept as a jaguar*. The forest becomes *savage with smoke and flame*. See the effect it has on the boys, even on Ralph.

Just before they realise the little boy is missing, a tree explodes in the fire and the creepers look like snakes as they burn. This is an example of a **symbol**: a thing which represents an abstract idea. ❂ With what do you associate snakes? What did the serpent do in the Garden of Eden? Is the island good, as Ralph says? You've already looked at the suggestion of evil and destruction. ❂ How does the imagery and symbolism in the description add to your idea of the island and its inhabitants?

Your turn now!

Now you've reached the end of the chapter, take a little time to think about Ralph's leadership. Record your thoughts in a Mind Map, starting with these branches:

strengths   **weaknesses**   **possible problems**

Do you think they were right not to choose Jack? What about Piggy? Does he show any qualities that would make him a good leader?

now you've seen the power of fire, take a break before a conflict of priorities

Chapter 3   Huts on the Beach

Learning to hunt

(To p. 53, … *just sufficient to bring them together again.*)

◆ Jack hunts a pig – doesn't kill it.
◆ Ralph talks about shelters and rescue.
◆ Jack talks about hunting and killing.
◆ Simon goes off by himself.

The description of Jack as a hunter makes him seem like an animal himself. We see him crouching, dog-like, and sniffing the air. Look at the way his appearance has changed. He's almost naked and carries a sharpened stick which he uses as a spear. ✪ What do you think about Jack's compulsion to kill a pig?

Already there is a clash of interests on the island. Although everyone promised to work hard to build the shelters Ralph has had to do most of the work himself, with the help of Simon. The others find activities like bathing, playing, and hunting much more appealing. ✪ What does Ralph feel about this? Notice the way Jack doesn't hear what Ralph is saying because he is entirely focused on hunting. Ralph is bewildered and angry that he can't make Jack see how important it is to build shelters and to be rescued, and Jack is frustrated and angry as he tries to communicate his compulsion to track and kill. ✪ Which do you think is the more important priority – hunting or building shelters? Can you find more than one reason for building the shelters as soon as possible?

Ralph and Jack communicate more easily when they talk about the littluns' fear. Notice that it's Simon who suggests that it may not be a good island. Even though Jack dismisses this idea he says he sometimes knows how they feel. ✪ What does Jack sometimes experience in the forest?

Your turn!

Before you go on, take 10 minutes to think about Ralph and Jack. Although they clash they do like each other, and are similar in some ways. Use the first three chapters to help you make some notes under these headings, or make a Mind Map. One similarity is shown to start you off.

	Jack	**Ralph**
Similarities	Wants to be leader	Wants to be leader
Differences		

Simon's secret place

(From p. 53, *Simon, whom they expected,* to end of chapter.)

◆ Simon goes to a secret place in the forest.

Simon helps to pick fruit for the littluns before going off on his own. Look at the way he responds to the island's sounds and smells. He is at home in its natural world, although he has just suggested that it may not be a good island. ✪ How is Simon's view of the island different from Ralph's and Jack's?

STYLE AND LANGUAGE

The description of Simon's secret place creates a strong sense of the island's vibrant colours and rich smells. Read the following extract and insert the missing words. The complete extract is printed at the bottom of the page.

The whole space was walled with dark_____ bushes.
Evening was advancing towards the island; the sounds of the
_____ _____ birds, the bee-_____, even the _____ of the
gulls were fainter. The slope of the bars of _____ sunlight
decreased; they slid up the bushes, passed over the green
_____ buds. With the fading of the light the _____ colours
died and the _____ tips of the flowers rose _____ to meet the
open air.

Something for you!

Use some of the details from this passage and information from
the first three chapters to begin a Mind Map of Simon's
character. Add to it as you work through the book. You could
do the same for the other main characters.

you should now understand some of the
themes of the novel. Take a break before
going on to the next chapter when things
start to go wrong

The whole space was walled with dark **aromatic** bushes.
Evening was advancing towards the island; the sounds of the
bright fantastic birds, the bee-**sounds**, even the **crying** of the
gulls were fainter.
The slope of the bars of **honey-coloured** sunlight decreased;
they slid up the bushes, passed over the green **candle-like**
buds. With the fading of the light the **riotous** colours died
and the **white** tips of the flowers rose **delicately** to meet the
open air.

Chapter 4   Painted Faces and Long Hair

New life, old life

(To p. 61, *The mask compelled them.*)

◆ Adapting to the new life.
◆ The littluns play.
◆ Some older ones spoil their play.
◆ Jack paints his face.

Look at the way reality is distorted on the island as the midday heat creates strange mirages and illusions. The cool of the night is welcome but the littluns in particular are scared in the dark. They are very dirty and have constant stomach aches because they eat fruit, often bad fruit, most of the day. ✪ At home, who would have been responsible for their appearance and health? Do you think anyone on the island should take this role?

When Roger and Maurice deliberately kick down the littluns' sandcastles Maurice feels uneasy and guilty. When Roger throws stones at Henry he aims to miss. Think about how they are still influenced by the rules which governed behaviour at home. Here we see how violence is restrained by memories of how people should behave. ✪ What might happen if these memories become weaker, and there are no authorities to enforce laws of behaviour? What does this suggest about the nature of human beings? Do you think that people behave in a civilised way only because they are forced to by laws and commandments? Perhaps this is true of only some people. What do you think – is our basic instinct to be thoughtful and protective, or to be cruel and self-gratifying?

Jack paints his face with clay and charcoal for camouflage when hunting, but the mask he creates has a powerful psychological effect as well. The sight of his mask fills him with awe and excitement. Notice how it changes Jack. His laughter becomes *bloodthirsty snarling* and he is *liberated from shame and self-consciousness*. With the mask to hide behind Jack is now free to behave in a violent, savage way. This is an important turning-point in his development.

Your turn!

Take some time now to think about all the changes in the boys' appearance since they arrived on the island. Draw a flow chart to help you track the changes that take place in their clothing and personal appearance and the effect these changes have. You could use words and pictures to record your ideas. If you like you could choose a few characters and draw up a separate chart for each. One on Ralph has been started for you.

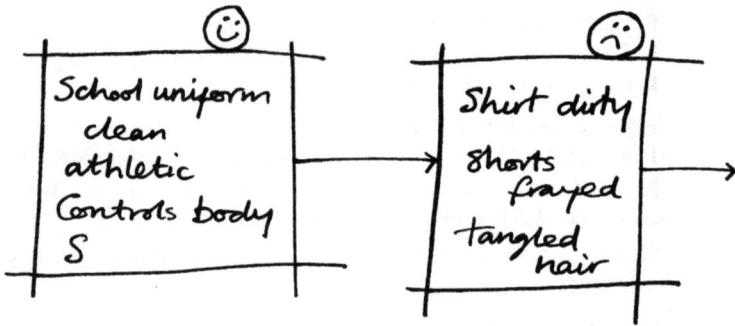

☺

School uniform
clean
athletic
Controls body
S

☹

Shirt dirty
Shorts
    frayed
tangled
    hair

now take a short break before looking at how the boys miss being rescued

It's a ship!

(From p. 61, *Ralph climbed out of the bathing pool*, to p. 65, '*There they are.*')

◆ Ralph, Piggy, Simon see smoke from passing ship.
◆ Signal fire has gone out.
◆ Ship passes.

Ralph laughs at Piggy when he talks about making a sundial, but Piggy thinks he's being friendly. He longs to be accepted by Ralph, but Ralph and the others see him as an outsider.
❂ You've already looked at some of the differences between Piggy and Ralph. Why does Piggy continue to be an outsider?

Ralph is in an *agony of indecision* when he realises the fire may have gone out. ❂ What decision does he have to make? What is he thinking and feeling? When they see the dead fire, Simon is in tears and Ralph is angry and bitter. The sight of the hunters returning in triumph makes it much worse.

Hunting or rescue

(From p. 63, *A procession had appeared*, to p. 68, *pushed down the plastered hair*.)

◆ The hunters return.
◆ Procession and chanting.
◆ They carry the slaughtered pig.
◆ Jack and Ralph clash.

Jack is excited and triumphant. He is both thrilled and disturbed that he cut the pig's throat. He wants Ralph to share the excitement and to praise him. Look at the way he justifies having let the fire go out. The idea that they have lost their chance of rescue doesn't seem important to him. ❂ What are Jack's feelings at this point?

Ralph blames Jack for being irresponsible and tries to make him realise the results of his behaviour. ❂ What are Ralph's feelings at this point? The two boys are worlds apart as they confront each other. Their feelings and their ideas about what is important are completely opposed.

'My specs!'

(From p. 68, *Piggy began again*, to p. 70, *... grabbed the glasses back*.)

◆ Jack hits Piggy.
◆ He breaks Piggy's glasses.

When Piggy blames Jack for letting the fire go out, Jack hits him in the stomach then on the head, breaking Piggy's glasses. Ralph has also blamed him. ❂ Why doesn't he hit Ralph? Jack gains support by mocking Piggy's response so that everyone laughs, and by offering a formal apology. Notice that it's Simon who gives back Piggy's glasses. ❂ What does Simon feel about what is going on?

The real struggle for power is between Ralph and Jack. Ralph wins the next round by refusing to move so that the fire has to be built a little way off. When Ralph borrows Piggy's glasses to light the fire he shows that he is now linking himself with Piggy and distancing himself from Jack.

More for you to do!

Take 10 minutes to think about the feelings and behaviour of Jack and Ralph. Why have Ralph's feelings about Piggy changed? What effect might this have on his leadership? In what ways is Jack a threat to Ralph? Should Ralph have given him control of the choir in the first place?

have a short break before reading to the end of the chapter and seeing how the hunting ritual begins

'I got you meat!'

(From p. 70, *Before these fantastically attractive flowers,* to end of chapter.)

- ◆ The pig is roasted.
- ◆ They act out the hunt.
- ◆ Ralph decides to call an assembly.

Jack's refusal to give Piggy meat is a display of power, weakened by Simon's kindness as he gives Piggy his portion. This makes Jack furious. He wants to be seen as the provider of meat and he wants them to understand the tactics and the skill that went into killing the pig.

Jack and the hunters act out the kill. Look at how the killing is celebrated and turned into a formal ceremony, a ritual. Some of the elements of the ritual remain the same as it is repeated throughout the book, and others change.

Check this!

Use the checklist below to help you identify what happens on each occasion and to trace the development of the ritual. Tick the columns where they occur.

	Chapter 4	Chapter 7	Chapter 8
procession			
dance			
chant			
circle			
offering			
person acting pig			
pig hurt			
pig killed			
person hurt			
person killed			
only 'hunters' involved			
others involved (name)			
How disturbing do you find it on a scale of 1–5 (1=low)?			

Golding tells us a lot about the characters through the way they speak. Can you identify who speaks the following phrases?

Them fruit   Your dad   My father   yah – Fatty!
Wizard   Stand still!   Daddy taught me
We don't want you   Golly!

take a break before tackling Chapter 5

Chapter 5: Beast from Water

'Things are breaking up'

(To p. 78, *What sunlight reached them was level.*)

◆ Ralph prepares for the assembly.
◆ He is very critical of their behaviour.

This assembly is very important for Ralph. He needs to show that he is in control, and to remind the boys of the things they should be doing. Look at how difficult Ralph finds it to think clearly and make the right decisions. He now respects Piggy, who is able to think things through. Ralph's values are changing. ✪ What does Ralph feel about his changed appearance? Remember to add to your flow chart.

Ralph is forceful and passionate as he tries to make the boys see how they have been behaving. He is disturbed by their lack of responsibility and co-operation, and the way they think rescue doesn't matter if they are enjoying themselves. He tells them there are certain things they must actually do, instead of just talking about them.

Ralph is strong enough to carry on even when he is interrupted. He addresses the question of the fear. He tells them they can deal with it if they talk about it rationally. He knows things are breaking up and not working, and wants to put it right. He wants them to be happy.

✪ What do you learn from Ralph's speech about the assemblies they've had? How have people behaved during them? What has happened to the decisions they agreed on? How are the boys responding to Ralph's leadership?

Maybe it's only us

(From p. 78, *Jack stood up*, to p. 85, *… shrank away defenceless to his seat.*)

◆ Jack, Piggy and Ralph and Simon talk about the fear and the beast.
◆ The littluns' nightmares.

Jack sees the fear as something you have to put up with, but declares that there aren't any beasts on the island. As he says later, if there is a beast, he and his hunters will kill it. Piggy takes a 'scientific' view and says that there's no reason for fear. He mocks the idea of ghosts and a beast; they have no place in Piggy's world of grown-ups and common sense. However, notice that he does say that people can make other people scared.
❍ Who do you think Piggy might have in mind here?

Piggy is right, but only partly. It is Simon who has the deepest recognition. Look at how he feels compelled to speak in the assembly, although he has to summon up his courage to do so. Simon sees the fear as something inside themselves, the evil that is in all human beings, not just the flawed ones like Jack.
❍ Why does Jack humiliate Simon when he tries to explain what he means? Remember to add to your Mind Map of Simon.

The littluns believe that the fear is caused by a beast that is *big and horrid*, that comes out of the sea, or is a ghost.
❍ Why do you think they need to project their feelings onto something physical?

'Bollocks to the rules!'

(From p. 85, *At last the assembly was silent*, to p. 88, … *beyond night-sight.*)

◆ The assembly disintegrates.
◆ Ralph calls for a vote on ghosts.
◆ He loses control of the assembly.
◆ Jack refuses to obey the rules.
◆ Jack leaves.

The talk about beasts and ghosts and the descending darkness unsettles the assembly. Ralph thinks it was a mistake to call the assembly so late. ✪ What do you think? He realises the fear is deep-rooted and can't be beaten by common sense. We can feel Ralph's despair as he feels the world of sanity and lawfulness slip away, and remembers that the ship has gone.

Piggy's outburst is an appeal for reasonable, civilised, grown-up behaviour. Jack's response, calling Piggy a *fat slug*, shows Jack's absolute rejection of these values. Look at the way Jack challenges Ralph's right to be leader, then dismisses the rules, and breaks up the assembly. ✪ What do you think makes Jack behave like this?

Three blind mice

(From p. 88, *Ralph found his cheek touching the conch*, to p. 90, … *powerless to help him.*)

◆ Ralph thinks he ought to stop being chief.
◆ Piggy and Simon want him to continue.
◆ There are now two separate groups.

Look at the way Ralph thinks his way through how to deal with this situation. Piggy still has faith in the conch. ✪ Why does Ralph decide not to blow it? There is a strong contrast between Piggy's talk of houses and streets and the boys who are dancing and chanting in the distance. Piggy recognises that Jack hates him and Ralph, and that Ralph is Piggy's protection. ✪ Why does Piggy have a greater understanding of people than Ralph does?

Scared and miserable, they long for a sign from the adult world. They long for the adult authority that would make everything all right. Do you think it would? ✪ Are things breaking up because there are no adults on the island?

Think about

Think about the way order has broken down on the island. Number these extracts from the novel in the order in which they appear, and where appropriate, say who is speaking.

I got the conch! Just you listen!
The rules are the only thing we've got.
Let's have a vote!
We've got to have rules and obey them.
Piggy was standing cradling the great cream shell.
Bollocks to the rules!
Jack held out his hand for the conch.
We'll have rules! Lots of rules!
Jack clamoured among them, the conch forgotten.
We ought to have more rules.

take a short break – before a beastly encounter!

Chapter 6: Beast from Air

'We've seen the beast!'

(To p. 96, *Jack called them back to the centre.*)

◆ Pilot parachutes from an air battle.
◆ His dead body carried to the mountain top.
◆ Body constantly moves as breeze tugs parachute strings.
◆ Sam and Eric go to relight fire, see figure, think it's the beast, and tell others.

The dead airman is a reminder that the adults are still fighting each other. ✪ What does this make you think about Piggy's conviction that adults would sort things out? In Sam and Eric's imagination the figure has become a beast with claws which chased them and nearly caught them. The boys now have a specific figure to focus their fear. ✪ Now they believe that the beast is on the mountain top, what could happen to the fire?

Over to you!

Take 10 minutes or so to think about the part Sam and Eric have played in the story so far. Jot down some of the things you have learnt about them. How strongly do they support Ralph? Is there anything special about them, or do you see them as basically decent and 'ordinary'?

when you've thought about Sam and Eric, take a break before finding out what the boys decide to do about the beast

'We don't need the conch any more'

(From p. 96, *This will be a real hunt*, to p. 98, *We'd better take spears.*)

◆ They decide to hunt the beast.
◆ Jack and Ralph clash.
◆ Ralph insists on relighting the fire.

Notice the continued conflict between Jack and Ralph as Jack again rejects the rules they've made. Ralph shows his sense of responsibility as he thinks about the littluns and Piggy, but Jack sees this as Ralph favouring Piggy. ✪ Can you think of another time when Jack showed his resentment of Ralph's friendship with Piggy? Ralph manages to stand up to Jack's challenge and maintain the leadership by reminding them all of the importance of being rescued. Although they're scared, they have to light the fire on the mountain. Again we are reminded of the different priorities of Jack and Ralph.

✪ Look at how Ralph agrees to explore the end of the island before going up the mountain. Why does he agree to do this? Do you think it's a good idea?

'What a place for a fort!'

(From p. 98, *After they had eaten*, to end of chapter.)

◆ Ralph, Jack and Simon set out with the biguns to hunt the beast.

◆ Simon doesn't believe in this beast.

◆ On the way they explore the tail-end of the island.

Notice that Ralph lets Jack lead the way, but when they cross to the castle he says that as chief he should go first. He is aware of the others watching him from behind. Then Jack is right behind him, saying he couldn't let Ralph do it alone. ❂ Is he being considerate? Look how excited Jack is by the castle rock. He and the others waste time by rolling rocks, and want to stay there instead of going on. Ralph has to struggle to remember that he's angry with this behaviour because they're forgetting the importance of the fire; something flickers in his mind, stopping him from thinking.
❂ Who helps him at such times? Look at the way the boys are muttering *mutinously*. ❂ Does anyone support Ralph? We can see his grasp of the leadership becoming very weak.

Simon can't believe in the kind of beast the twins have described. He understands that the real beast is in human beings.

Look both ways

The section you have just read looks backwards and forwards. It reminds us of the first time the boys explored the island, and foreshadows Piggy's death on Castle Rock. ❂ What differences do you see between this exploration and the first one? What aspects of this incident foreshadow Piggy's death?

before finding out how Ralph gains some status, take a break

Chapter 7   Shadows and Tall Trees

'You'll get back all right'

(To p. 110, *and everybody laughed*.)

◆ Ralph broods and daydreams as they continue their search.
◆ Simon comforts him.
◆ Ralph spears a boar.
◆ They act out the attack.

Ralph feels disgusted at their dirty, neglected appearance. He is dismayed that he now accepts this unpleasant condition as normal. Notice that they are now on the other 'unfriendly' side of the island, where Ralph feels *helpless* and *condemned*. Here the view is harsh, the sea is cold. Here Ralph finds it hard to believe in rescue.

Simon reassures Ralph that he'll get back all right. ❂ How does he know how Ralph is feeling? Do you agree with Ralph that Simon is *batty*? Simon is seen by them all as an outsider, like Piggy. Like Piggy, he has important things to say. Ralph has learnt to take Piggy seriously, but he dismisses Simon. ❂ Can you think of any reasons for this?

Ralph's daydream about home tells us more about his background. Look at how the details he brings to mind create a sense of comfort and security. In his mind he goes back to a time when his mother was still there and his father was home every day. He thinks about the last house he lived in before being sent away to boarding school. ✪ Why does Ralph think longingly of home at this particular point? What kind of life was he used to?

There is a dramatic contrast between Ralph's dreams of a time that was *good-humoured and friendly* and the sudden crashing movement as the boar breaks cover. Ralph is full of *fright and apprehension and pride* when he realises that his spear hit the pig. Look at the way he enjoys the respect he has won and feels that hunting is good after all. For a moment Ralph shares some of the hunters' feelings. ✪ Does this surprise you? Ralph gains respect when he spears a pig, but not when he insists on the importance of living in a civilised way while looking for rescue. ✪ What does this tell you about the values held by the boys? When Ralph joins in the mime afterwards he jabs at Robert and feels the desire to *squeeze and hurt.* ✪ What has brought out these feelings in Ralph?

Ralph does feel uneasy about the mock hunt and says it was *'just a game'*, like rugger. It makes him feel better to see the experience in these terms, but there are differences between this mime and a game like rugger. ✪ What similarities and differences can you see?

Your turn!

Spend a little time adding to your flow chart tracing their changing appearance. You could also add to your Mind Map of Simon at this point, and fill in the 'ritual' checklist.

take a break – before some terror!

Something like a great ape

(From p. 110, *Ralph sat up,* to end of chapter.)

◆ They go up the mountain.
◆ Simon goes back to join Piggy.
◆ They see the parachutist.
◆ They're terrified and run back down.

The bitter struggle for leadership between Jack and Ralph continues, as Jack tests and taunts Ralph, and Ralph responds to his goading. Again we see Ralph thinking through the decisions he has to make, and considering the position of the littluns and Piggy. Again we see Jack's resentment of Ralph's concern for Piggy. Ralph understands that as soon as Jack stops leading he becomes antagonistic towards him; Jack just can't cope with Ralph being in charge. Ralph brings out into the open Jack's hatred for him. His question *'Why do you hate me?'* makes everyone feel awkward. ✪ Why do they feel uneasy? Piggy has said that Jack hates both him and Ralph. What do you think Jack's feelings for Ralph are?

The conflict between Jack and Ralph here is based on accusations of cowardice. Jack throws out the challenge to Ralph to climb the mountain and Ralph responds with a show of cool bravado. Ralph is influenced by Jack's mockery to act against his better judgement. ✪ Should they have gone on in the dark? Can you think of another occasion when darkness affected their reactions?

Simon has gone back to be with Piggy so isn't there when they reach the top of the mountain. Notice that he doesn't mind going through the forest by himself. ✪ Who else is at home in the forest? Is it for the same reason? Think about what might have happened if Simon had been with them when they climbed the mountain.✪ Do you think he would have seen the dead parachutist, or the beast? Why did the others see the beast and not the parachutist?

STYLE AND LANGUAGE

You have read Golding's descriptions of the island's wonderful features like the beautiful lagoon, the palm-fringed shore and the warm dark green beach pool. In this chapter he describes the other side of the island. Look at the harsh words like *hard, clipped blue* and *the brute obtuseness of the ocean*. The friendly side of the island is expressed with words like *defended, shield, quiet*. There, it was possible to dream of rescue. Here, Ralph feels *clamped down* and *helpless*. The opposing feelings of safety and rescue and those of hopelessness and despair are expressed through the contrasting language.

Now try this!

It isn't just the island that has different sides. Think about the boys. Are they entirely good or entirely bad? Look at this circle of 'good' and 'bad' characteristics. Choose words to put in each character's circle.

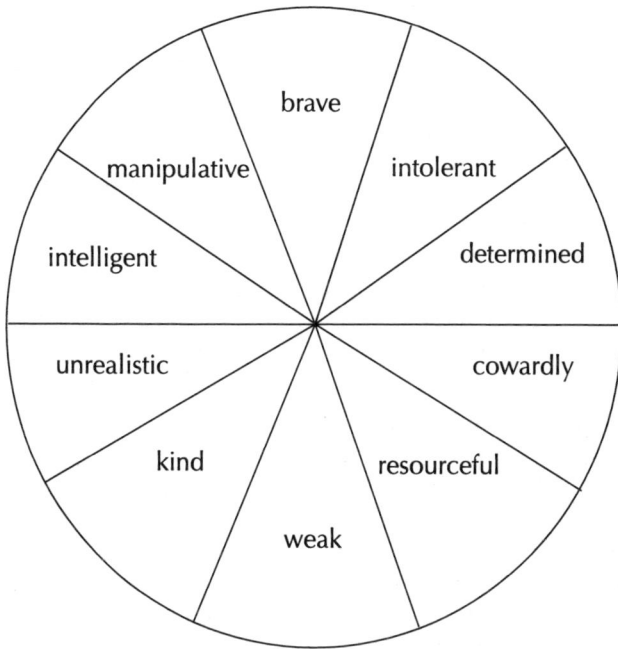

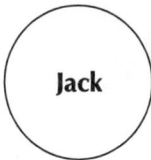

by now you should have your own ideas about the 'beast'. Have a break before finding out more in Chapter 8

Chapter 8: Gift for the Darkness

Jack's assembly

(To p. 122, *Ralph watched him.*)

◆ Ralph and Jack report back to the others.
◆ Jack challenges Ralph for the leadership.
◆ He loses the vote and leaves.

Ralph is in despair. He feels that the figure on the mountain top has beaten them. They are terrified of it, they can't fight it, and so they will never be able to light the fire that is their only hope of rescue. The beast has destroyed their chances. ❂ Is their hope of rescue weaker now? If it is, is it the fault of the figure on the mountain?

Jack is stung by what he sees as an insult to his hunters. He tells the assembly that the beast is a hunter – notice that unlike Ralph he doesn't talk about the implications for rescue. He uses the mood of fear and uncertainty to launch an attack on Ralph's right to be chief.

Key points from Jack's criticism of Ralph

coward   not a hunter   not a prefect   not known to them
gives orders   expects obedience   talks too much

❂ Which, if any, of Jack's criticisms do you think are valid?

Jack feels angry and humiliated when the boys don't vote for him. Look at the way he offers them the chance to join him when he hunts. He says Ralph can catch his own pigs, but knows that won't happen. Think about the appeal of what Jack offers. His world of hunting and eating meat is satisfying both physically and emotionally. The hunt and the kill provide the excitement and solidarity which is very different from Ralph's world of tedious duty and routine, and the meat is a welcome change from the boring, bland diet of fruit. A little later Piggy and even Ralph are tempted by the roast meat. ✪ Do you blame those who choose Jack instead of Ralph?

We can do all right on our own

(From p. 122, *Piggy was indignant,* to p. 127, *He continued to sit.*)

◆ Simon thinks they should climb the mountain.
◆ Piggy suggests building the fire near the platform.
◆ They notice lots of hunters have gone to Jack.
◆ Simon goes off by himself.

Everyone laughs at Simon when he says they should climb the mountain. ✪ Are you surprised at their reaction? Simon's answer, that it is the only thing to do, shows the depth of his awareness. He understands that the only way they can rid themselves of the fear and live in peace is to confront what scares them and understand it. Look at the description of Simon in his private den when he pauses on his way up the mountain. He is preparing for the journey he is about to make for the sake of other people's lives. ✪ Can you link Simon with others in history and myth who sacrificed themselves for the truth?

Piggy is very relieved at Jack's departure. Still hiding behind Ralph's position, he speaks with new authority and assurance. His suggestion to move the fire shows his intelligence. His new confidence can be seen in the way he helps to build the fire, and for the first time lights it. Piggy thinks it was Jack spoiling things. ✪ Is Jack to blame for everything that goes wrong, or are there events which are not directly his fault?

Do you think Piggy's common sense could make things better on the island?

Think about the feast of fruit that Piggy and the twins bring to comfort Ralph. ✪ How is this different from the feast Jack shortly has?

Look at the way Ralph doesn't realise that he's tugging at his nail and making it bleed. Piggy has to remind him of the importance of the smoke signal. These are further signs of Ralph's deterioration, of the way he is cracking under the strain, and of his need for Piggy.

Think about

Before you go on to the next section of the chapter take 10 minutes or so to think about Piggy. What aspects of his character and behaviour do you admire? Is there anything about the way he thinks and behaves that you find hard to admire? Think about Piggy's leadership qualities. Are there any circumstances in which Piggy would be a good leader? Are there any ways in which he is in fact leading them now?

treat yourself to a short break, then prepare for some bloodshed!

This head is for the beast

(From p. 127, *Far off along the beach*, to p. 131, *through the forest towards the open beach*.)

◆ Jack appoints himself chief.
◆ They kill a sow feeding her piglets.
◆ The pig's head is left on a stick as a sacrifice to the beast.

Jack is *brilliantly happy* now he is leader. Look at the way he becomes chief. ✪ What does this suggest about the way Jack will rule? He declares his strategy: he will get more of the biguns on their side, kill a pig, have a feast and leave some of the kill for the beast. Think about how different this is from Ralph's plans. The boys follow Jack *obediently*. ✪ Why do they find it easier to obey Jack than Ralph?

Jack tells them that they can forget the beast because their offering will placate it. The hunters respond fervently to the declaration that they can stop the beast bothering them, and that they won't dream so much at this end of the island.
❂ What seems to be the appeal of Jack's style of leadership?

The killing of this pig is an important turning-point. They spear a sow who is suckling her piglets. The killing is brutal and horrific, and the violence almost sexual. At the beginning Jack claimed that they had to hunt for meat. We also saw the impulse to control and overpower a living being. Now there is thick excitement and fulfilment in the killing, the disembowelling and the decapitation. Look at the way Jack rubs blood on Maurice's face. Think about how the ideas and customs of civilised society have been forgotten. Leaving the pig's head as a sacrifice is a primitive action.

Notice that Jack is addressed as 'Chief' from now on.
❂ What is the effect of the use of this title instead of his personal name?

What makes things break up?

(From p. 131, *Simon stayed where he was*, to p. 136, *sudden gust of hot wind*.)

◆ Simon sees the killing and the pig's head.
◆ Ralph and Piggy talk about the breakup of their society.
◆ Jack and his tribe steal sticks from their fire.
◆ Jack invites them to a feast.

Simon's hiding place is different from the peaceful, beautiful retreat it was. As he faces the pig's head with the flies and the spilled guts, even the butterflies desert him. He has a conversation with what Golding calls the 'Lord of the Flies'. This is a translation of Beelzebub, a biblical name for the Devil. Look at the way he hears the head telling him to run away, to go back. ❂ Is he really hearing another voice, or is it his own? Does it matter? If Simon had gone back, he wouldn't have been killed. We see how he shades his eyes from the sight, then eventually meets the pig's gaze. He is building up to his final confrontation with evil. He feels an *ancient, inescapable recognition.* ✪ What do you think Simon recognises?

Notice how the *close, tormenting* heat builds up as we prepare for the thunderstorm, and Simon's tension also builds up as a pulse begins to beat in his brain.

Keep track

This is a long chapter and a very important one. Take a few minutes to work on your Mind Map of Simon.

take a short break before going on to the rest of the section

We see Ralph struggling to understand why the others don't see the importance of the smoke signal. Look at the way he finds it hard to think *like a grown-up*, and loses his thread of thought as he tries to remember what he should say about the fire. Once more Piggy has to prompt him and remind him of the connection between fire and rescue. Again we have the sense of a shutter flickering in Ralph's brain. Notice that his long *idiot* hair is a real irritant and almost seems to obstruct his thinking as it gets in his eyes. We've already been told that he would like to cut his *filthy* hair, and it is often referred to as a *mop*.

As we see throughout the book, there is a very close connection between the boys' physical state and their psychological or mental state. Jack's hunters are now painted, anonymous savages. Their sticks are spears. These hunters once sang in unison in the choir; now, at Jack's insistence, they talk in unison in a frightening ritual designed to enhance Jack's power and authority.

Piggy was sure they had come for the conch. ✪ Does Jack think the conch is at all important now? Ralph's group regards the conch with *affectionate respect.* ✪ What does this tell you about the difference between the two groups?

We should notice that what Jack promises seems attractive to them all, even Ralph. He says he would like to put on war-paint and be a savage. ✪ What is it that makes Ralph stand out against the attractions of Jack's way of life?

The Lord of the Flies

(From p. 136, *You are a silly little boy*, to end of chapter.)

◆ Simon has an imaginary conversation with the Lord of the Flies.

Simon feels *one of his times* coming on. ✪ What other references are there to Simon having experiences like fainting fits? Sometimes people with a condition like epilepsy have unusual experiences in which they have strange or different perceptions of the world. ✪ Is this one of Simon's fits, or is it a visionary experience?

WHAT THE VOICE SAYS

Simon hears the voice offering him different alternatives. It tries to humiliate him, telling him he's just a silly little boy and he should run away and play. It refers to his friendship with Ralph and Piggy and Jack, and suggests how much easier Simon would find things if they accepted him and didn't think he was *batty*. Look at the way Simon stands up to the voice and states what he knows is true, that what he is facing is a pig's head on a stick. ✪ Would it be easier for Simon to join the others and believe in the beast? The voice in Simon's head tells him that the real beast is inside them all. It takes on the tones of a schoolmaster warning him that he is just a *poor misguided boy* and will suffer if he tries it on, if he speaks out. Everyone, Ralph and Piggy included, will *do* him. Look at the range of tactics the voice uses: mockery, threats, promises to *forget the whole thing*.

SIMON'S REACTION

Simon loses consciousness, maybe through the effort of fighting these suggestions and keeping to what he knows is the truth. ✪ Think about the parallels you have found in Simon's life and the lives of prophets or saints. Simon's experience with the Lord of the Flies echoes the Bible story of Christ being tempted in the wilderness. Like Christ, Simon uses all his strength to resist and will continue on his journey to reveal the truth to others and so save them.

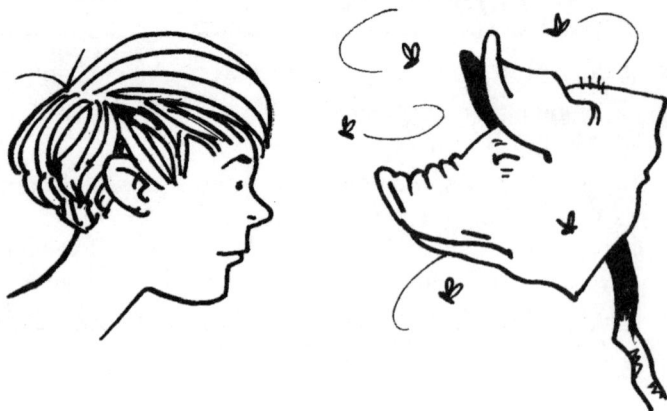

⌨ *STYLE AND LANGUAGE*

Look at the way Golding uses the language of the schoolboy
world of play and games to show their increasing savagery.
Many playground games involve fun and ritual. Jack's hunting
offers both these elements. We see how the game of miming
the hunt begins playfully and develops viciously. Notice how
everybody laughs when Jack says they should use a littlun for
the part of the pig.

The childish language of school and the playground highlights
the grim reality of what is at stake on the island. One of Jack's
criticisms of Ralph is that he isn't even a prefect. ✪ Is this an
appropriate comment in the circumstances? When he loses the
vote he says he's not going to play with them any more, or be
part of Ralph's lot. ✪ How do these comments affect the way
you see Jack? This kind of language reminds us that these are
small boys with very little experience of the world outside. ✪
What does this suggest about human nature?

How do they compare?

Use the chart at the top of the next page to help you identify
the boys' different attitudes to the beast. One or two suggestions
have been filled in. You could use illustrations and symbols as
well as words. If you like you could Mind Map the information.

	Ralph	Piggy	Simon	Jack	Others
What it is			man		
Where it is					
How it can be overcome				kill it	

Add to your Mind Map of Simon.

before looking at Simon's bravery, take a break

Chapter 9   *A View to a Death*

Simon finds the body

(To p. 141, *Ralph squirted water again.*)

◆ Simon reaches the mountain top.
◆ He frees the dead airman.
◆ He starts back down the mountain to tell the others.
◆ Ralph and Piggy decide to go to Jack's feast.

Notice the way we feel the storm building up so that the air is ready to explode. There is no refreshment in the air, no beauty in the surroundings. The sense of relentless pressure is felt in Simon as well as he climbs the mountain. He feels he has no choice in the matter, but walks *drearily* and with *glum determination*. He could have taken the easy way out, but he knows he must do what he's set out to do. ❷ Do you think Simon is brave? Some of the others have shown courage. ❷ Is Simon's courage the same as theirs?

Simon sees *a humped thing suddenly sit up* and sees the remains of the *poor body*. ❷ Why does Simon see this, when the others had seen the beast? Look at the way he examines the figure closely to make sure he understands what it is, although the sight and the smell makes him vomit.

Simon performs another act of kindness and compassion when he loosens the parachute lines to set the figure free from its

55

indignity. His final act of service to others is to go back down and tell the boys that there is nothing to fear from the figure on the mountain. ✪ Why is it important for them to understand this?

We see the continued build-up of the storm as Piggy inspects the *looming sky* and complains about the pain in his head. ✪ Why do Ralph and Piggy decide to go to Jack's feast? Notice the irony of Piggy's statement that they ought to go to make sure nothing happens.

Painted and garlanded

(From p. 141, *Long before Ralph and Piggy,* to p. 144, *'Come on! Dance!'*)

- ◆ Jack is presiding over his feast.
- ◆ Ralph challenges his leadership.
- ◆ The storm breaks.
- ◆ Jack orders them to dance.

Jack seems like a primitive god, throned on a log with a garland around his neck, surrounded by offerings of food and drink. He gives orders which the boys obey, and conveys warnings which they heed. Jack now has the power he wanted. Notice that his power is based in the physical threat suggested by the *brown swell of his forearms*. His authority is said to chatter *like an ape*. ✪ Will Jack use authority responsibly? Jack sees himself as a good leader, their protector and provider of food. ✪ Is this enough?

Ralph insists that he is still chief, and refers to the democratic way he was appointed. He also claims the authority of the conch, but Jack rejects it. We see Ralph speaking *tremulously* and *breathlessly*. ✪ What does this tell you about the way he feels and the position he's in? Ralph says he'll blow the conch. ✪ Who would go to the assembly?

Ralph is momentarily in a good position when the storm breaks and he points out their lack of shelters – but notice that Piggy has had to remind him that he should talk about the fire and rescue. Jack's response as the lightning flickers and the thunder rolls is to order everyone to dance. ✪ What is the purpose of the ritual dance at this point?

Think about

What kind of leader has Jack become? What are the similarities and differences between this Jack and the Jack who led the choir at the beginning? What are the main differences between the way he leads and the way Ralph leads? Take 10 minutes to work on your notes or Mind Map of Jack.

now have a short break before you go on to read about Simon's death

Simon is killed

(From p. 144, *He ran stumbling*, to end of chapter.)

◆ The storm rages.
◆ They act out the hunting ritual.
◆ Simon crawls out of the forest.
◆ In their frenzy they see him as the beast.
◆ They batter Simon to death.
◆ Simon's body is carried out to sea.

This time the mime is frenzied and frightening, lit by flashes of lightning in the *dark and terrible* air. Ralph and Piggy join in, feeling a kind of security in being part of the ritual. Look at the way the dance develops, with Roger being the pig then moving out of the circle leaving the centre empty. They stamp and chant as if the rhythmic repetition will keep them safe. ○ Why do they chant *'Kill the beast!'* instead of 'Kill the pig!'?

Simon staggers into the circle of savage, dancing boys. He tries to tell them the truth about the 'body on the hill', that there is nothing to fear from it, but is beaten to death as he speaks. His words bring to mind the crucifixion, when Christ died on the hill of Calvary. ○ What do you feel about Simon's death? Could he have saved himself? Do you think he should have done?

As Simon dies, a great wind blows and carries the parachute and the body of the dead parachutist out to sea. This completes Simon's act of compassion in releasing the body by freeing the parachute lines from the rocks. The dead airman is a victim of inhumanity, like Simon.

Simon's body huddles on the beach until the tide changes and it is carried out to sea, like the airman's. Notice the way Simon seems to become absorbed into the natural world, which he loved so much, and to become part of the universe. He is transformed from the pathetic broken body into something beautiful and majestic. Look at the contrast between the dignified ceremony of his burial, presided over by nature, and the ferocious, vile ritual which caused his death.

STYLE AND LANGUAGE

The description of Simon's burial is strikingly beautiful. Look at the way Golding creates a sense of the rhythm and majesty of the universe with phrases like *Somewhere over the darkened curve of the world the sun and moon were pulling* and *while the solid core turned*. Simon's torn body is transformed. The line of his cheek is silvered and his shoulder becomes *sculptured marble*, suggesting coolness and endurance. Notice the brightness around his hair. ○ What kind of people are traditionally painted with an aura of light around their heads? Simon is escorted by bright moonbeam-bodied creatures who guide him on his way. The calm solemn language which describes how Simon becomes part of eternity challenges the brutal ugliness of the way he died.

Your turn!

You should now take 10 minutes or so to add to your Mind Map of Simon. What is your final judgement of him?

have a rest before considering how the boys cope with what they've done

Chapter 10   *The Shell and the Glasses*

Murder or accident?

(To p. 150, *We left early.*)

◆ Ralph and Piggy discuss Simon's death.
◆ Only Sam and Eric and a few littluns left.

Ralph's small group is a pathetic reminder of the previous assemblies. They meet on the platform and Ralph cradles and caresses the conch.❷ Why does he laugh when Piggy suggests he should call an assembly? What is he feeling?

Ralph says that what they did was *murder*. He feels a mixture of loathing, feverish excitement and fear. Look at the physical reminders of the attack. ❷ You could add these to your appearance flow chart. He says that he is frightened *of us.* ❷ What does this suggest to you about Ralph's view of the beast? Who else felt like this? Notice that Ralph tries to face up honestly to what they did, and to accept guilt and responsibility.

Piggy doesn't want to face the truth. He finds excuses for what has happened. He says they were scared and anything might have happened, that Simon might have been pretending, that it was an accident, that he asked for it anyway. ✪ Why does Piggy come up with so many excuses? Piggy has spoken a lot of sense before now, and he has also faced some truths. Here, however, he is dishonest, deceiving himself and trying to deceive others. Simon died because he wanted to tell the truth and save others. ✪ Do you think he *asked for it*?

We see the twins' guilt in the way they go red and explain that they got lost last night. They all shake convulsively at the memory of the *obscene* dance none of them attended. Note how Golding's irony makes us aware of the guilt they all feel but can't acknowledge.

Rule by fear

(From p. 150, *When Roger came to the neck of land*, to p. 153, *Again the murmur swelled and died away*.)

◆ Jack rules Castle Rock.
◆ He warns the beast may come again in disguise.
◆ They plan a raid to steal Piggy's glasses.

Look at the strategies Jack's tribe uses to make itself feel strong. The huge rock is poised at the entrance to the 'fort', ready to be used as a weapon. They use military language like *Halt!* and *Advance*; they are called *defenders of the gate*. Jack's face is completely obliterated by white and red clay. The original purpose of the mask was to provide camouflage. ✪ What is the effect and purpose of Jack's paint? Think about Jack's decision to beat Wilfred. ✪ What does it tell you about Jack's use of power? How do you think power should be used?

Jack has to deal with his tribe's guilty memories of the night before. Notice the way they refer to Simon as the beast. This is their way of distancing themselves from the reality of what they have done. ✪ How is it different from the way Ralph's group do this? When Jack tells them that they couldn't have killed the beast they feel relieved. ✪ Why do they feel like this? At the same time they feel daunted at the thought that the beast may terrorise them again, but Jack assures them that they can keep on its right side by leaving it the head of their kill. If they meet it again they can do their 'dance'. ✪ What does this suggest about their future behaviour? Jack recognises their fear and promises a feast. ✪ How well do you think Jack deals with the situation?

Over to you!

Take a little time now to think about the part Roger has played in the story. Look at the way he behaved in Chapter 4 and the part he played in killing the sow in Chapter 8. What effect does Jack's decision to beat Wilfred have on him? Think about the way his sadistic impulses are kept in check at the beginning, then released into deliberately cruel behaviour. Draw a Mind Map of Roger, and add to it as you work through to the end of the book.

have a short break before you go on with this chapter

'He was a chief now in truth'

(From p. 153, *Piggy handed Ralph his glasses,* to end of chapter.)

◆ Ralph, Piggy, Sam and Eric try to keep the fire alight.
◆ Ralph has nightmares.
◆ Jack's group attacks.
◆ Ralph and Eric end up fighting each other by mistake.
◆ Jack takes Piggy's glasses.

Ralph wants to keep the fire alight for comfort and to provide a signal. Notice that this is the first time he's admitted the need for comfort. However, a little later he forgets what is good about a fire and has to be prompted by Piggy. The curtain flaps in his brain and stops him thinking. ✪ Who is the strongest and steadiest at this point? Look at the way Ralph sniggers when Piggy says they've got to be rescued soon or they'll be *barmy.* ✪ What is Ralph feeling? Do you think Piggy is right?

When Ralph dreams of home he imagines holidays in Devon, but now he finds the wildness of Dartmoor and the ponies disturbing instead of attractive. ✪ Why does Ralph need to *'suppose'* every night? His dreams of a normal, safe town and bus station become a nightmare as he starts to dance around a lamp post and a strange bus crawls out of the bus station. ✪ What event does this dream recall? What does it tell you about Ralph's feelings?

The fight is described as *vicious*. There are snarls, bites, scratches. ✪ What is the effect of these words? In the darkness and confusion, Ralph and Eric fight each other. Think about the options that Jack and his group had. ✪ Did they need to launch this kind of raid? What else could they have done? Once again Piggy thinks they have come for the conch. ✪ Why didn't they take it?

Your turn!

Before you go on to the next chapter, draw together all your ideas about Piggy's glasses. Why does Jack now feel he is *a chief now in truth*? Piggy's glasses are a trophy as well as a practical aid. Think about their importance throughout the novel. Jot down some ideas about the part they play and what they represent. You could make a Mind Map of this. Piggy is now unable to see. What are the implications of this?

chapter 11 begins with a desperate assembly. Before that, take a break

Chapter 11: Castle Rock

'I got to get my glasses back'

(From p. 160, *In the short chill of dawn*, to p. 165, ... *for the first time.*)

◆ Ralph calls an assembly.
◆ A few littluns, Piggy, Sam and Eric are there.
◆ They decide to visit Jack to get back Piggy's glasses.

The tiny assembly still uses the conch. ✪ Why do they do this? Notice that it is described as *fragile*. ✪ What does this suggest? Piggy still has great faith in the conch and is proud to carry it. He believes that Jack will respect its authority and that he will respond to an appeal to do what's right. Piggy is fired with moral outrage and indignation, which gives him the courage to face Jack. He now acknowledges that Simon was murdered and that the child with the birthmark must be dead. At the same time, notice that he is weak in other ways now. He has to be led *like a dog* and helped to his food. ✪ Is Piggy being realistic about the approach to Jack?

Ralph is full of despair and anger. He speaks passionately about the fire and their inability to keep it going, but loses the thread again and has to be helped by Piggy. Ralph gets angry when Piggy has to prompt him again about the smoke. ✪ Why does Piggy always let Ralph take the lead, and remind him that he's chief?

Ralph wants to tidy up their appearance before confronting Jack. He thinks that reminding them of the standards they used to have will persuade the savages to behave in a civilised way. Ralph says *'We'll be like we were.'* ✪ Can they ever be like they were?

Sam and Eric realise that Ralph is losing his grip. Also, they are very scared of Jack, and intimidated by the warpaint the savages wear. ✪How strong do you think they are? Why have they remained loyal to Ralph?

Take a closer look

Think about your reactions to Piggy. There are probably times in the book when you admire him, times when you feel irritated by him, times when you feel sorry for him. Your feelings might be the same or different from those of the other characters. Take 10 minutes to identify your feelings at particular points. A possible reaction to the section you've just read is filled in.

Event	What I feel	How strongly I feel it	Comment on others
Asking for his glasses back	Admiration for his courage not sure about outcome	Very	Ralph is persuaded

We've come to say this

(From p. 165, *They set off along the beach*, to p. 169, *There may be a ship out there*.)

◆ They approach Castle Rock.
◆ Confrontation between Ralph and Jack.

Ralph's group seems small and pathetic as they make their way to the fort. Notice that Piggy holds the conch *carefully* as he is guided on his way by the shadow of the twins' wooden spears. We are reminded of Simon's death as they pass in silence the spot where he was killed. ❂ What is the effect of this ominous reference? Piggy is terrified as he feels his way on the narrow path high above the square of rock on which he will fall. This is an example of 'foreshadowing'.

Ralph's call for an assembly is met with silence and thrown stones. Think about the time earlier in the novel when Roger threw stones, aiming to miss. ❂ How is the atmosphere different now? Does Roger feel the same restraint which controlled him before? Ralph tries to belittle the savages, calling them *painted fools*, and appeals to their sense of honour, telling them they're not *playing the game*. He fails to realise quite how savage they have become.

Ralph is fired with righteous indignation as he demands to have Piggy's glasses back, and shows courage in standing up to Jack. Look at how the fight between them starts when Ralph calls Jack a thief. ✪ Is this the worst thing he could call Jack? Is the fight just about this? Notice how at this point they don't use the pointed ends of their spears. Even though Piggy is clutching the ground in terror high above the sucking sea he still reminds Ralph of the reason they came to the fort, and prompts him about the fire. However, talk about the fire and rescue means nothing to the others.

Piggy's death

(From p. 169, *He paused, defeated by the silence*, to p. 172, *the body of Piggy was gone*.)

◆ Jack orders Sam and Eric to be tied up.
◆ Ralph and Jack fight.
◆ Roger dislodges rock.
◆ Piggy is killed.

Jack responds to Ralph's plea for sense by ordering Sam and Eric to be tied up. ✪ Why does he do this? Look at how excited the *painted group* becomes as they grab the twins and feel power over them. This is the same excitement they feel when killing pigs.

In the middle of Ralph and Jack's fight Piggy holds up the conch and demands to be heard. The tribe does fall silent. ✪ Why do they listen to Piggy? What sound accompanies Piggy's words? For the last time Piggy asks for rational, civilised behaviour as the rock dislodged by Roger hurtles towards him. The conch is shattered at the same time. *The talisman, the fragile, shining* shell is smashed into a thousand white fragments. Notice that Piggy and the conch he loved and respected to the end are destroyed together. The conch has represented the values of democracy, responsibility and order, ideas which Piggy steadfastly upheld. ✪ What is the importance of Piggy's death and the destruction of the conch? Is there any hope left for the boys on the island?

STYLE AND LANGUAGE

You have already looked at the kind of language Ralph uses when he confronts Jack and the tribe. There are other examples of words and phrases which seem inappropriate in the circumstances. For instance, Sam and Eric protest *Oh I say!* and *Honestly!* The language of middle-class schoolboys sounds odd and jarring in this place of violence and murder. This sort of language reflects a world which has disappeared and standards which no longer exist.

Compare the description of Piggy's death with that of Simon. Phrases like *stuff came out and turned red* and *Piggy's arms and legs twitched a bit* are harsh and ugly. Whereas Simon's body achieved beauty and dignity in its slow movement out to sea, Piggy's is suddenly gone, sucked into the bloodstained water. ✪ Why do you think there is such a difference in the two descriptions?

Ask yourself

What is your final judgement of Piggy? What strengths and weaknesses did he show? What do you think about his death? Could it have been avoided? Remind yourself of the important things Piggy said and did on the island.

take a short break before the final descent into savagery

The hangman's horror

(From p. 172, *This time the silence was complete*, to end of chapter.)

◆ Jack hurls his spear at Ralph.
◆ Ralph wounded – escapes into forest.
◆ Roger prepares to torture the twins.

Look at the behaviour that is unleashed by Piggy's death. Jack threatens Ralph with the same kind of fate as Piggy and deliberately throws his spear at him. Roger intervenes when Jack starts to prod Sam with a spear to force them to join the tribe. He indicates that he knows a more effective form of torture, and pushes past Jack to get at the twins. He now has a *nameless authority*. ❂ What kind of authority does Roger have? Think about a possible change in his status since he sent the rock flying to kill Piggy. Think about the taboo which stopped him aiming to hit Henry, all that time ago. ❂ Are any of the boys still governed by those old ideas of right and wrong?

Chapter 12   Cry of the Hunters

Ralph and the Lord of the Flies

(To p. 176, *whoever it was up there had a spear at the ready*.)
◆ Ralph alone and hiding in the forest.
◆ He heads towards Castle Rock.
◆ He comes face to face with the skull of the pig's head.

Ralph is like an animal who is being hunted. He is injured and filthy, starving and terrified. Look at the way he tries to convince himself that they will leave him alone, and tries to see the Bill who once wore shorts and a shirt in the striped savage he sees from his hiding place. However, he knows that Jack will never stop pursuing him. ❂ What is the *indefinable connection* between Ralph and Jack? What does Jack need to destroy?

Ralph responds to the pig's skull with *fear and rage*. When he tries to destroy it its grin seems to get wider. Think about Simon's experience with the pig's head. Simon accepted its message and what it stood for, and accepted that evil was present in everyone. ❂ Can Ralph accept this? Why does he lash out at the figure? Why can't he destroy it?

A stick sharpened at both ends

(From p. 176, *He knelt among the shadows*, to p. 181, *... a dark interior slope*.)

◆ Sam and Eric warn Ralph that he will be hunted.
◆ Roger has sharpened a stick at both ends.
◆ Sam and Eric are tortured for speaking to Ralph.

Ralph realises that he's an outcast. He says he is isolated just because he had some sense. ❂ Who does this remind you of? His sense of isolation is made worse when he realises that Sam and Eric are part of the tribe and are guarding the rock against him. They have been tortured into a *new and shameful loyalty*. ❂ Do you blame them for joining Jack? Notice that Eric tells him to never mind what's sense – that's gone. Ralph has to face the fact that there is now no trace of the old world of laws and reason. There is nothing left to appeal to. ❂ What do you think Ralph must feel like at this point? What do you think the twins feel like?

Picture a stick sharpened at both ends. Ralph has to struggle to understand its significance. He is in fact carrying such a stick, the one he pulled out of the pig's skull to use as a spear. ❂ What will the stake be used for when they catch Ralph? Think about what they did with the head of the pig they had killed, and what they did with the rest of the body.

Ralph is now an outsider, just as Simon and Piggy were. ❂What is it about the behaviour and attitudes of each that makes him an outcast? Are there any similar reasons for their isolation? Are there any important differences?

Smoke!

(From p. 182, *He was awake before his eyes were open*, to p. 188, *... sharpened at both ends*.)

◆ Ralph wakes to the sound of the hunters.
◆ Sam and Eric have revealed his hiding place.

◆ Jack sends rocks crashing down.
◆ He realises Jack has set the forest on fire.

Ralph feels secure and clever in his thicket, even when he realises they know where he is. Look at the way he fingers the point of his spear and imagines a savage stuck on it, *squealing like a pig.* ❂ What is happening to Ralph? He gnaws the bark of his spear without realising it and bites his fingers; he shows his teeth and snarls. When he attacks the savage he launches himself like a cat, and stabs and snarls. Ralph is being hunted like an animal and is reacting like a terrified animal at bay. We see him trying to work out which is the best of three choices. ❂ What are they? Try to picture an image to represent each one.

Ralph tries to hold on to sense and reason, but dreads the curtain flickering in his brain again. From the hiding place he worms his way into, he hears the sound of the fire, and notices that his spear has two sharp ends. ❂ Do you think Ralph realises what they intend to do with him? Notice that even at this dreadful moment we see Ralph's basic responsibility as he wonders what the tribe will eat if they burn the fruit trees.

STYLE AND LANGUAGE

This chapter is written in such a way as to bring us right inside Ralph's head, so that we identify with his thoughts and feelings, and experience them in the same way he does. Notice how the short sharp sentences show his breathless panic and his attempts to think clearly:

Break the line.
A tree.
Hide, and let them pass.

The style of this passage makes us a part of Ralph's attempt to consider his options. It is an effective and dramatic way of enabling us to share Ralph's thoughts and emotions.

The rescue

(From p. 188, *The savage stopped fifteen yards away*, to end)

◆ Ralph is spotted and surrounded.
◆ He breaks out and runs to the open beach.
◆ He collapses and cries for mercy.
◆ A naval officer is standing over him.
◆ The savages come forward.
◆ Ralph breaks down in tears.
◆ The others sob.
◆ The officer waits for them to pull themselves together.

The tension increases as the savage peers into the thicket and Ralph looks straight into his eyes. There is an explosion of action as Ralph shoots forward and runs for his life. We hear the roar of the fire and the cries of the hunters as Ralph becomes *hopeless fear on flying feet*. Look at the way he falls down and holds up his arm to protect himself. ✪ What does he expect to happen? What does the reader expect?

There is a startling and dramatic change of perspective when we suddenly see the figure of the naval officer. We see the scene through his eyes. Instead of savages about to kill Ralph, we see a semicircle of little boys. The officer sees Ralph as a *little scarecrow*, the smaller boys have the *distended bellies of small savages*. They look as if they've been playing some kind of game. Their bodies are streaked with coloured clay, and a red-haired boy has the remains of a pair of spectacles at his waist and the remains of a strange black cap on his head. ✪ What do you feel when you see them from this point of view?

Think about the faith they used to show in the adult world. Here at last is the ship they had longed for and a representative of the adult world of order and civilisation. Look at the submachine gun, the revolver. ✪ What kind of world are the boys returning to? Are the world of the island and the world outside very different from each other?

Notice the irony of the officer's comment *Fun and games* and his jocular *Nobody killed, I hope?* ✪ Do you blame him for not understanding the situation? He reprimands them for not having done better, saying that British boys should have put up a better show. He refers to *Coral Island*, one of the story books the boys mentioned at the beginning, in which the stranded boys behave sensibly and co-operatively. He expects that children will behave in a reasonable and responsible way. ✪ Does he have a realistic view? Notice that in the end it is smoke which brings about their rescue, but this smoke is from a fire intended to destroy, not save.

Ralph weeps in pain and grief for all they have lost. He recognises their loss of innocence and *the darkness of man's heart*, and weeps for Piggy, his true wise friend who died defending civilised, responsible behaviour. Ralph has learnt about the evil that is in everyone. He knows now that human beings are essentially flawed. He now has to live with this knowledge.

Look at the officer's embarrassment at their tears as he waits for them to pull themselves together. Although he is engaged in war, and looks at the *trim 'cruiser'*, ready for action, he knows less about the real meaning of war and the real nature of humanity than Ralph does.

Your final impression

What do you think about the ending of the book? Does the rescue seem like a fairy-tale ending? Think about the overall impression it has made on you. Is its effect pessimistic, or not?

now you should understand the story, the characters and the main themes. Use these ideas as starting-points for a Mind Map of the whole book!

TOPICS FOR DISCUSSION AND BRAINSTORMING

One of the best ways to revise is with one or more friends. Even if you're with someone who hardly knows the text you're studying. You'll find that having to explain things to your friend will help to organise your own thoughts and memorise key points. If you're with someone who has studied the text, you'll find that the things you can't remember are different from the things your friend can't remember – so you'll be able to help each other.

Discussion will also help you to develop interesting new ideas that perhaps neither of you would have had alone. Use a **brainstorming** approach to tackle any of the topics listed below. Allow yourself to share whatever ideas come into your head – however silly they seem. This will get you thinking creatively.

Whether alone or with a friend, use Mind Mapping (see p. v) to help you brainstorm and organise your ideas. If with a friend, use a large sheet of paper and thick coloured pens.

Any of the topics below could feature in an exam paper, but if you think you've found one in your actual exam, be sure to read the question carefully and to answer the precise question given.

TOPICS

1 At the end of the book Ralph thinks of Piggy as his *true, wise friend*. Do you agree with this view of Piggy?
2 Write about the struggle for power between two characters in a book of your choice.
3 Choose two of the following settings in *Lord of the Flies* and discuss their importance in the book as a whole: Castle Rock, Simon's secret place, the mountain top, the meeting place.
4 Which character in *Lord of the Flies* do you most admire? Write about the character's part in the book and show what he does and says that makes you admire him.

5 Choose two incidents from *Lord of the Flies* in which Golding has presented different atmospheres. Write about each and discuss how the different effects are created.

6 Choose a scene or extract from a book you have studied which you think is very important to the book as a whole. It might be important because it adds to your understanding of character, or it might be central to the book's theme. Write about the extract you have chosen and show why it is important.

HOW TO GET AN 'A' IN ENGLISH LITERATURE

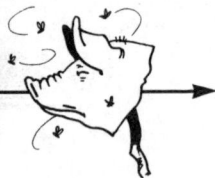

In all your study, in coursework, and in exams, be aware of the following:

- **Characterisation** – the characters and how we know about them (e.g. what they say and do, how the author describes them), their relationships, and how they develop.
- **Plot and structure** – what happens and how it is organised into parts or episodes.
- **Setting and atmosphere** – the changing scene and how it reflects the story (e.g. a rugged landscape and storm reflecting a character's emotional difficulties).
- **Style and language** – the author's choice of words, and literary devices such as imagery, and how these reflect the mood.
- **Viewpoint** – how the story is told (e.g. through an imaginary narrator, or in the third person but through the eyes of one character – 'She was furious – how dare he!').
- **Social and historical context** – influences on the author (see 'Background' in this guide).

Develop your ability to:

- Relate **detail** to **broader content, meaning and style**.
- Show understanding of the author's **intentions, technique and meaning** (brief and appropriate comparisons with other works by the same author will gain marks).
- Give **personal response and interpretation**, backed up by **examples** and short **quotations**.
- **Evaluate** the author's achievement (how far does the author succeed and why?)

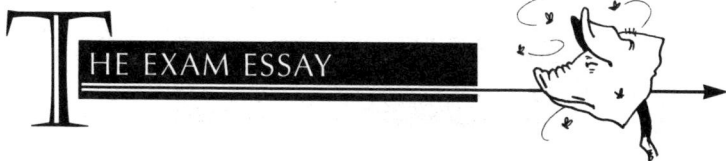

THE EXAM ESSAY

Planning

You will probably have about an hour for one essay. It is worth spending about 10 minutes planning it. An excellent way to do this is in the three stages below.

1 **Mind Map** your ideas, without worrying about their order yet.
2 **Order** the relevant ideas (the ones that really relate to the question) by numbering them in the order in which you will write the essay.
3 **Gather** your evidence and short quotes.

You could remember this as the **MOG** technique.

Writing and checking

Now write the essay, allowing five minutes at the end for checking relevance, and spelling, grammar and punctuation. Do remember to **stick to the question**, and always **back up** your points with evidence in the form of examples and short quotations. Note: you can use '. . .' for unimportant words missed out in a quotation.

Model answer and plan

The next (and final) chapter consists of a model answer to an exam question on *Lord of the Flies*, together with the Mind Map and essay plan used to write it. Don't be put off if you think you couldn't write an essay as good as this one yet. This is a top 'A' grade essay – a standard at which to aim. You'll develop your skills if you work at them. Even if you're reading this the night before the exam, you can easily memorise the MOG technique in order to do your personal best.

The model answer and essay plan are good examples for you to follow, but don't try to learn them off by heart. It's better to pay close attention to the wording of the question you choose to answer in the exam, and allow Mind Mapping to help you think creatively.

Before reading the answer, you might like to do a plan of your own, then compare it with the example. The numbered points, with comments at the end, show why it's a good answer.

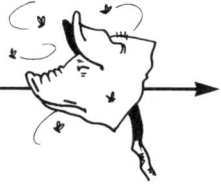

M ODEL ANSWER

QUESTION

Describe how Ralph changes in the course of the novel, and show why these changes occur.

PLAN

1 Beginning – confident schoolboy.
2 Popular leader.
3 Attitude to Jack – likes at first.
4 Clashes with Jack over hunting and fire.
5 Can't understand why Jack hates him.
6 Attitude to Piggy – friendship.
7 Respect for Piggy grows.
8 Mourns Piggy's death.
9 Deteriorates – can't think; dirty; like animal.
10 Lost innocence.
11 Learns about human nature – evil and brutality.

ESSAY

At the beginning of the novel Ralph appears mature and confident. He is delighted to be stranded on this glamourous island, and is sure that his father will rescue them.[1] He tells Piggy his father is a commander in the navy and asks Piggy what his father is. It seems that Ralph takes his middle-class background for granted and assumes that others are the same as him. He has a tall athletic figure and 'attractive appearance' which is part of the reason he is chosen as leader.[2] He is pleased to be leader and is a popular choice. He deals well with Jack, making up for his disappointment at not being chosen by giving him charge of the choir. All these things change for Ralph.[3] His relationship with Piggy and with Jack changes, he learns more about other people, and he experiences horror on the island.

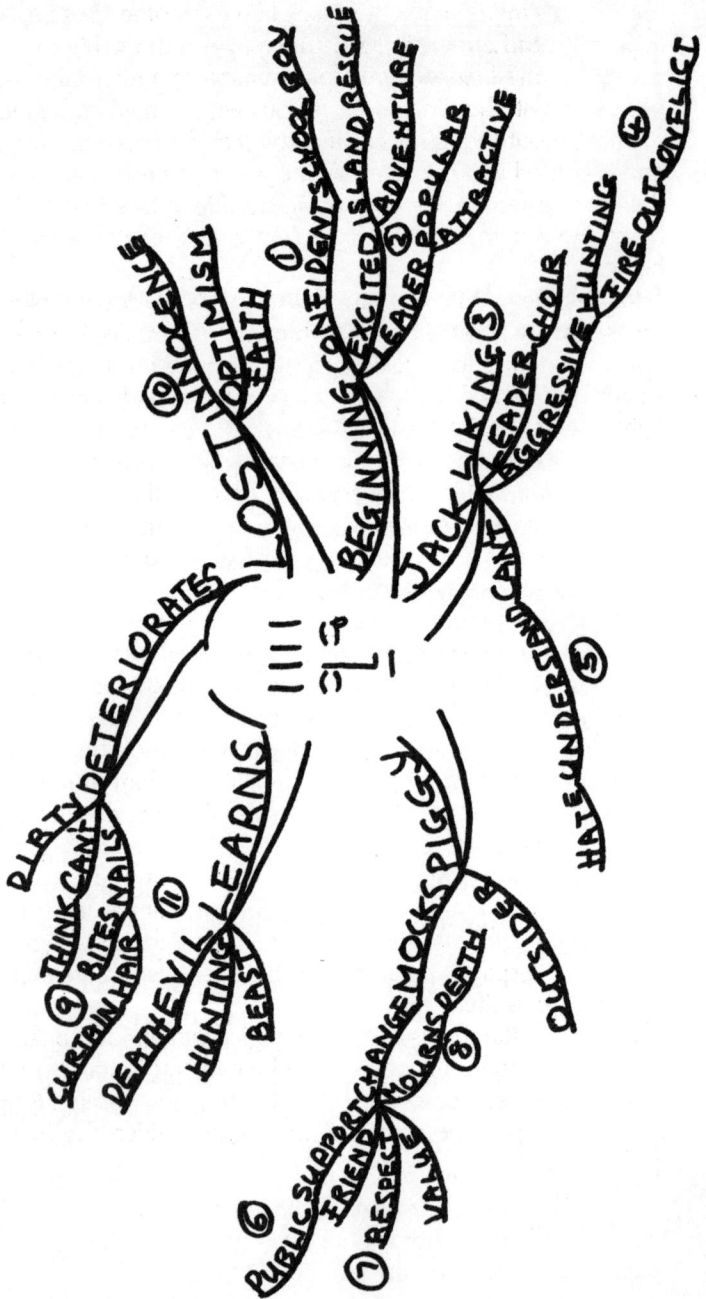

At the beginning Ralph and Jack like each other, but Jack's aggressive and domineering nature makes him unable to accept Ralph's leadership. Ralph is unable to understand Jack's obsession with hunting and is furious with him when he lets the fire go out.[4] Ralph is horrified by Jack's increasing savagery and is baffled and frustrated by the way he doesn't care about the fire and rescue. He ends up screaming at Jack that he is 'a beast and a swine' and has to accept what Piggy says, that Jack hates him.[5]

Ralph's view of Piggy changes. At first Ralph doesn't take him seriously and makes fun of him like the others, but he gradually comes to realise Piggy's good qualities. He publicly shows his alliance with Piggy when he borrows his glasses to light the fire.[6] Ralph has to change his values. His experience of being leader makes him understand the importance of clear thinking, and he learns to respect Piggy's intelligence.[7] He says 'Piggy could think. He could go step by step inside that fat head of his'. He also values Piggy's loyalty and in the end calls him his 'true, wise friend'.[8]

As the story progresses Ralph realises that things are breaking up. There is a series of disturbing events. The little boy with the birthmark disappears, everyone becomes frightened of the beast, only a handful of the boys agree with him about the importance of the rules and being rescued. Ralph becomes ashamed of his filthy appearance and we see him losing his grip as he unconsciously bites his nails and can't think straight.[9] Being a leader isn't as good as it seemed at first and Ralph begins to crack up under the strain. He becomes frightened and pessimistic and is not airily optimist about rescue as he was at the beginning. The deaths of Simon and then Piggy add to Ralph's despair until at the end he is reduced to an animal running for its life.

In the end Ralph has learnt the tragic truth about human nature. He knows that people can be evil and brutal. Even he has experienced some pleasure in hunting and hurting. Ralph will never again see life as he did that first golden day on the island.[10]

WHAT'S SO GOOD ABOUT IT?

1 Keeps question in mind – gets straight to point.
2 Good use of textual reference.
3 Shows firm grasp of question.
4 Uses example.
5 Shows development of relationship.
6 Shows knowledge of text.
7 Points well chosen.
8 Good use of quotation.
9 Good use of detail and example.
10 Shows high level of perception – gives clear answer to question.

GLOSSARY OF LITERARY TERMS

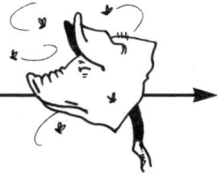

allegory   a story which has a literal meaning and a symbolic meaning.

context   the social and historical influences on the author.

dramatic irony   *see* **irony** (dramatic).

fable   a story with a specific moral or message, usually made up by one person (as in 'Aesop's Fables').

image   a word picture used to make an idea come alive; e.g. a **metaphor**, **simile**, or **personification** (*see* separate entries).

imagery   the kind of word picture used to make an idea come alive.

irony   (dramatic) where at least one character is unaware of an important fact which the reader knows about, and which is somehow hinted at.

metaphor   a description of a thing as if it were something essentially different but also in some way similar; e.g. *Small flames ... crawled away.*

myth   an ancient traditional story of gods and heroes, which has evolved over time, and which embodies popular ideas and beliefs.

personification   a description of something abstract as if it were a person.

simile   a comparison of two things which are different in most ways but similar in one important way; e.g. fire *like a bright squirrel.*

theme   an idea explored by an author; e.g. order.

setting   the place in which the action occurs, which usually affects the atmosphere; e.g. the two sides of the island.

structure   how the plot is organised.

viewpoint   how the story is told; e.g. through Ralph's eyes when he is being hunted.

INDEX

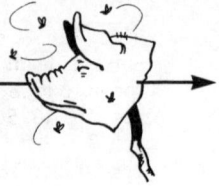

Page references in bold denote character or theme outlines.

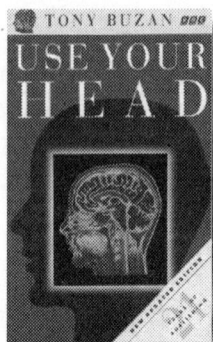

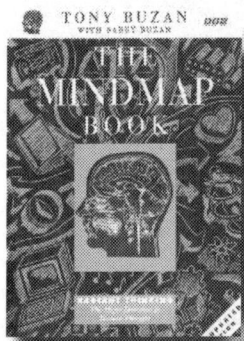